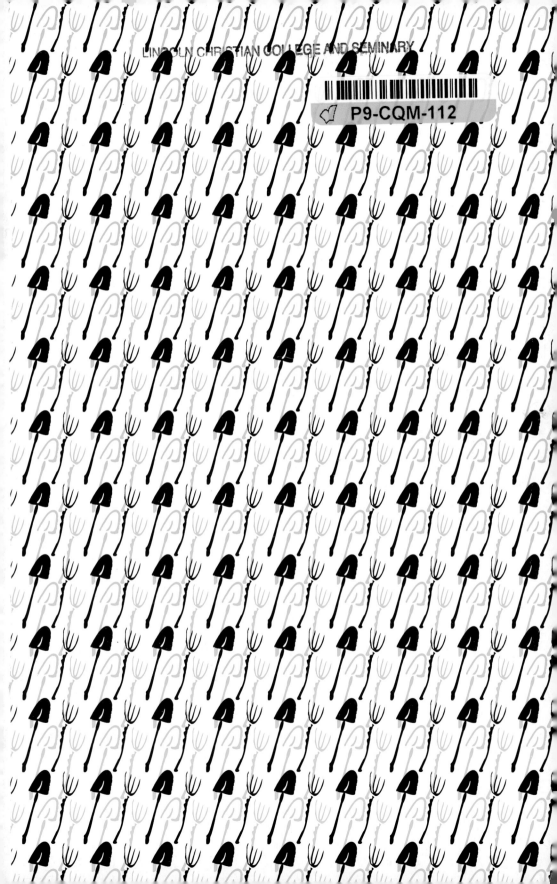

C Endpapers The func-
tional difference between
a shovel and a pitchfork is
the metal that is *missing*.

The Elements of Graphic Design

Space, Unity,
Page Architecture,
and Type

Alex W. White

ALLWORTH PRESS
NEW YORK

"Graphic design has become such a central part of our Post-modern visual language that it has developed into a carrier of meaning at least as significant as the words and images it is presenting. For this reason Post-modern white space becomes a very significant void."
Keith Robertson in
Looking Closer: Critical Writings on Graphic Design

11 10 09 08   11 10 9 8

Published by Allworth Press
An imprint of Allworth Communications
10 East 23rd Street, New York, NY 10010

Book design, composition, and typography by Alexander W. White, New York, NY

Library of Congress Cataloging-in-Publication Data
White, Alex.
The elements of graphic design: space, unity, page architecture, and type / Alex W. White – 1st ed.
    p.   cm.
Includes bibliographical references and index.
ISBN-10 : 1-58115-250-7
ISBN-13 : 978-1-58115-250-0

1. Graphic design (Typography) 2. Layout (Printing) 3. Type and type founding. I. Title.
    Z246.W56 2002
    686.2'2–dc21

Printed in Canada

This book is concerned with what things look like, but supposes that *what is being said* is worth the effort of clarity.

"Design is not the abun-
dance of simplicity. It is
the absence of complexity."
Anonymous

The Elements of Graphic Design

Space, Unity, Page Architecture, and Type

Contents

Preface

In the course of writing and designing my previous book, *Type in Use*, I became intrigued by the study of white space, the dynamic emptiness that lies behind printed type and imagery. I became fascinated by the importance of white space and by the necessity of "not filling in all the space." This resulted in a lecture I delivered in New York in May 1992 titled *Page Design: What Works and Why*. My research into design's white space and abstraction completely changed my approach to consulting and teaching. They are essential to sophisticated and compelling designs. A designer who can handle white space and abstraction can handle more design problems because he has trained his mind to see form more accurately and critically.

Abstraction makes an idea clearer by removing unnecessary details. Abstraction can be harmful, though, when it obscures the message by removing identifiable markers. Discretion and judgment in its use are essential and are improved with practice and experience.

Unlike mathematics, where there can only be a single "right" answer, design has many alternate solutions. It is up to the designer to find the best among these. Design is not an opportunity to show off one's latest visual notions for one's colleagues. On the other hand, monotony is not good design either, even if the basic structure of that monotony is pretty. Why? Because sameness puts browsers to sleep. Good design balances deliberate consistency with flexibility so *some* of the goodies will stand out. Designers are in service to their readers by accelerating learning and making content stick.

Design – whether graphic, industrial, interior, or architecture – is the process of taking unrelated parts and putting them together in an organized unit. Each discipline works with solids and voids and each must respond to three questions: What are the elements I have to work with? Where do these elements go? What structure is necessary so they go together?

A HARMONIOUS DESIGN REQUIRES THAT NOTHING BE ADDED OR TAKEN AWAY

ꓲ ꓲ ꓲ ꓲ ꓲ ꓲ

VITRUVIUS XC–XX BC

🎧 **Vitruvius foretold Step 3.** There is a huge difference between "nothing wrong" and "nothing right" about a design. Being able to identify what is right about one's work is crucial to organizing material for clarity. Merely having nothing wrong is no assurance that a design is successful in communicating. There must be something identifiably right in a design for it to achieve elegance.

↷ One definition of good design is the balance between monotony and the designer's self-indulgence.

This book is dedicated to Clare, who, like white space, is the glue that holds everything together.

Design is simple when you remember it is a *process*, not a *result*. ❶ Define the problem you have been given. This is usually a redefinition because you have been given an *apparent* problem. The redifinition must home in on the real issues. If you don't become clearer about how to handle the material, you haven't redefined the problem accurately enough.

❷ Know the material. Digest it fully. At the very least, read it.

❸ Distill the essential from the mass of confusing muchness. Nothing may be missing, and nothing may be extraneous. This is the definition of elegance.

❹ Abstract the main point so its importance to the reader is clear and it is visually arresting. A message that doesn't stop readers won't be read.

❺ Unify all elements so they don't outshout each other.

Thanks to:

■ Tad Crawford, Liz Van Hoose, and Nicole Potter, who are committed to quality and clarity. *And* they are sweet people with whom to work. ☐ Charla Honea, a writer and editor in Nashville, for calling me "spay-shul," when I told her about my plans for this book at its earliest stages. I misunderstood her to mean *special*. She meant *spatial*, which still makes me smile. Charla's insight, advice, and suggestions helped me immeasurably. ☐ Clyde Hanks for his encouragement at 6,000 feet. ☐ Elizabeth, Sneaux, Rosinha, and Isabela for making the office a much nicer place each day. ☐ Professor Larry Bakke, a student's hero. ☐ Carl Dair (1912-1967), a designer's hero. ☐ Neil Bittner, a teacher's hero. ☐ Stuart Schar, a professor's hero. ☐ Jan VW, der brüders' hero. You can ask them. ☐ And *now, I'm going to tell you something:* very special thanks and love to Lilian, who has given me the time to put ideas together into the book you are holding. I don't mean time we could have spent together, say, *spatziering* around Manhattan. I mean earning time. You are generous *end olzo* beautiful. *"Shut the door."*

Alex W. White

Alex W. White
New York City

Southern light and northern skill come together in a photographer's portraits of his two daughters.

North and South of the Equator

By Jean-Pierre Raffin

Photos by *Baden de Oliveira*

North
and South
of the Equator

Southern light and northern skill come together in a photographer's portraits of his two daughters.

By Jean-Pierre Raffin Photos by Baden de Oliveira

C Making the content a reader magnet The top layout is confusing because font use does not connect thoughts, there is a near total lack of alignment or connectedness between elements, the subhead's typographic "color" is uneven, and the empty space has been distributed evenly throughout the spread. The bottom example is more appealing and easier to read because connectedness has been created – things touch – leading the reader from one element to the next effortlessly. Also, a powerful display font has been used, the words have been placed in a pattern that reveals their natural order (including the subhead, which has been "broken for sense"), and some space has been purposefully left empty.

"Perfect communication is person-to-person. You see me, hear me, smell me, touch me. Television is the second form of communication; you can see me and hear me. Radio is the next; you hear me, but you don't see me. And then comes print. You can't see or hear me, so you must be able to interpret the kind of person I am from what is on the printed page. That's where typographic design comes in." Aaron Burns (1922–1991)

Introduction

Nothing puzzles me more than time and space; and yet nothing troubles me less, as I never think about them. – Charles Lamb (1775–1834)

To design means to plan. The process of design is used to bring order from chaos and randomness. Order is good for readers, who can more easily make sense of an ordered message. An ordered message is therefore considered *good design*. But looking through even a short stack of design annuals, you will see that what is judged *good* changes with time. It is apparent that style and fashion are aspects of design that cannot be ignored. Stephen A. Kliment, writing in an *Architectural Record* magazine editorial, advises, "Do not confuse style with fashion. Style is derived from the real needs of a client or of society. Fashion is a superficial condition adopted by those anxious to appear elegant or sophisticated." Leslie Segal, writing in the introduction to *Graphis Diagrams*, says, "Elegance is the measure of the grace and simplicity of the design relative to the complexity of its functions. For example, given two designs of equal simplicity, the one conveying more information is more elegant. Conversely, of two designs conveying the same information, the simpler is the more elegant. Inelegance is a frequent design failing."

A communicator's job

Having material on the page read and absorbed is a visual communicator's chief responsibility. The Xerox Corporation completed a landmark project by distributing their Xerox Publishing Standards (page 6). In it, they describe their design rationale: "The principal goals of page layout are visual recognition and legibility. These goals are accomplished through consistent typography, effective use of white space and graphics, and controlled use of [lines].... A repeated visual logic guides the eye and helps

EL PESO ES LO DE MENOS

Ellos dejaron de preocuparse por lo que les decía la balanza, se aceptaron tal cual son y se convirtieron en personas triunfadoras, en un mundo que parece pensar solo en los flacos

Por
Mariano
Romero

Tanto nos han invadido con el tema, que definitivamente estamos viviendo una obsesión con la figura. En un mundo en el que los flacos son el modelo de la perfección porque así lo ha dictado la moda, existen casos de personas que sobresalen, no solo por su figura generosa, sino por su talento y magnetismo personal. Si bien es cierto que ser gordo muchas veces implica marginación o suerte de rechazo, estos famosos que conversaron con Vistazo no se han dejado frustrar por la presión de las dietas

the reader scan. A generous amount of white space is reserved as a blank presentation area, allowing headings to 'pop out' and wide graphics to be extended."

It is important to make the page look inviting – a "reader magnet." Visual stimulation draws viewers into the page, arousing their curiosity and actively involving them in the process of absorbing information. Visual simplicity eliminates uneccessary elements and structures those that remain in a logical, consistent system. Good design reduces the effort of reading as much as possible, thereby encouraging readership and understanding.

Readers respond to consistent page structure. The job is *not* to fill in all the space in order to impress the reader with sheer quantity of information. That will just overwhelm the reader with overfullness.

Imagine coffee being poured in a cup. If the cup is filled to the very top, it is difficult to avoid spilling it on yourself as you take the first sip. By having *too much* of a good thing, we have created a problem. This is exactly the same reaction readers have to being given too much information at once. It is perceived as a problem and their response is to avoid it. Umberto Eco, the Italian author and professor of semiotics, writes about too-muchness in his description of William Randolph Hearst's castle in San Simeon, "The striking aspect of the whole is not the quantity of antique pieces plundered from half of Europe, or the nonchalance with which the artificial tissue seamlessly connects fake and genuine, but rather the sense of fullness, the obsessive determination not to leave a single space that doesn't suggest something, and hence the masterpiece of bricolage, haunted by *horror vacui*, that is here achieved. The insane abundance makes the place unlivable...." Again, the designer's job is not to fill in all the space. It is to make information accessible and appealing.

The best use of the page's empty space is to help make information scannable, not merely to make the pages pretty. That will automatically follow. The point is to increase the page's *absorbability*.

⌒ **What *not* to do with space** Society has not improved the landscape by overfilling it with construction. Neither does a designer improve a page by overfilling it with content.

"It is better to be good than to be original."
Ludwig Mies van der Rohe (1886–1969)

Ϲ **The design process expresses significance.** The design process is one of sifting through the less important to find the essential. This is done in stages, first by removing the large chunks of less valuable content, then looking through increasingly fine grades of information. Having at last identified the essential, designers enhance its significance for their readers.

C ∩ **Substituting form attracts attention** because it results in unexpected contrast.

∩ **Physical form conveys meaning.** Matching an element's form to its meaning helps reveal the message.

∩ **The stylized "Y" inside this logo** for a Finnish insurance provider is easily visible. But it takes a moment longer to recognize the "S" shape that represents the first half of the company's name, Suomi-Yhtiö.

The mind searches for meaning

As humans evolved, an important attribute we acquired was the ability to see potential dangers around us, to see differences in our surroundings. Anything that moved irregularly or was a different color or texture was worthy of our attention. After all, it might eat us. Noticing differences became an evoltionary advantage for humans. As a result, when we modern humans look at a printed document or a monitor screen, our eyes instinctively and subconsciously look for similarities and differences among the elements used. We search for the unique, which is determined by *relative unusualness*.

Design is like sifting through sand for seashells. The human brain sifts images and bits of type. It innately simplifies and groups similar elements. If it cannot easily make these connections, it perceives confusion. The majority of readers are disinclined to exert much effort in digging out the meaning or importance of a message. They may be too busy or they may be uninterested in the subject. Indeed, many readers subconsciously look for reasons to stop reading. It's demanding, hard work, it takes concentration, and we're all a little lazy. As has been said about advertising messages, "Tell me sweet, tell me true, or else my dear, to hell with you."

Designing is the process of looking for and showing off the similarities and differences inherent in the content of a visual message. This can sometimes take a good deal of time if the similarities do not immediately present themselves. But the search for similarities is at the heart of what a designer does.

In addition to searching for similarities and differences in our environment, we look for meaning in the physical form of the things we see. The form of a thing tells us certain things about itself. A couple of decades ago, Transformers® were introduced and quickly became a best-selling toy. Their popularity was based on the idea that an object could be disguised as something it is not. Designers struggle to reveal the meaning of their messages by using type, imagery, and space. If used well, the meaning is

illuminated and the process of communication is well served. If used poorly, the meaning is confused by poor choices or is subsumed by the prettiness of the message's presentation.

Successful designs describe the content fully and as simply as possible. This is the definition of *elegance.* Ideally, the reader should be unaware of the act of reading, for reading is then truly effortless. In design, more is *not* better. There must be an economy in using type and imagery, or marks of any kind. If it hasn't got a purpose (other than decoration, perhaps?), it shouldn't be used. Despite the abundance of busy, overproduced design work we've seen in recent years, the excellence of a design is in direct proportion to its simplicity and clarity.

Space attracts readers

LP records have a narrow space of relatively empty vinyl between songs. The songs share similar texture because the spiral groove

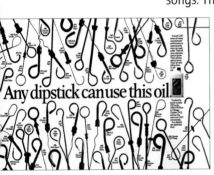

in which the needle tracks is tightly and consistently spaced. The space between songs is smooth, black vinyl interrupted by only a single groove. The visual dividers make it possible to count the number of songs and estimate their relative length, serving as cues when we make recordings from them. Digital media makes far more accurate information available, but it can't be seen by the naked eye on the disk itself.

The pauses between songs on a record show content the way white space does. Space attracts readers by making the page look accessible, unthreatening, and manageable. Leaving too little white space makes a page look crowded – *good only if that's the point you want to make.* Leaving too much white space is almost impossible. I say "almost" because you will get groans of disapproval if you toss around chunks of *unused* white space, that is, emptiness purely for its own sake, rather than for the

sake of the message. Readers are less likely to notice or object to too much white space than to an unreadable, crowded page.

Readability is a term that refers to the adequacy of an object to attract readers. It should not be confused with *legibility*, which

Buy Sevin® SL for this.   Get these free.

White Grub

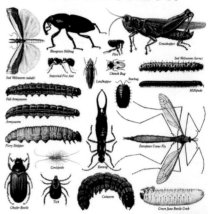

Bluegrass Billbug · Flea · Grasshopper · Sod Webworm (larva) · Sod Webworm (adult) · Imported Fire Ant · Chinch Bug · Leafhopper · Sowbug · Millipede · Fall Armyworm · Armyworm · Fiery Skipper · Centipede · Earwig · European Crane Fly · Chafer Beetle · Tick · Cutworm · Green June Beetle Grub

Your reasons for choosing a turf insecticide could be summed up in two words: Kills grubs.

Which, frankly, is reason enough to choose SEVIN® brand SL carbaryl insecticide. Because, when it comes to grubs, no other turf insecticide is more effective.

We have the efficacy data to prove it.

But if that still isn't enough to make you a confirmed SEVIN® brand SL user, consider this:

With SEVIN® brand SL carbaryl insecticide, you also get effective control of 27 other turf pests.

Including tough ones, like chinch bugs, billbugs, armyworms, cutworms, and sod webworms.

And SEVIN® brand SL carries a Toxicity Category III Caution label. Which makes it ideal for use on golf courses, parks, lawns, or any turf area frequently used by people and animals.

So ask your turf chemicals supplier for SEVIN® brand SL carbaryl insecticide. It may be the best example yet of getting more than what you pay for.

From the turf care group at Union Carbide.

Clinton's next test: selling tax increase

Associated Press

WASHINGTON — The newest test effort to pass a relatively competitive spending bill, President Clinton faces a tougher fight on his next challenge: persuading Congress to approve the biggest tax increase in history.

This time, the Senate rules are in the favor. Republicans cannot block a vote on the tax-and-spending package.

Still, Clinton may have to fight to muster enough quorum measures to spend $16 billion for emergency jobs.

On the other hand, Clinton's tax bill must command allies on taxes — the Senate and House Ways and Means and Senate Finance committees — are committed to preserving the broad outlines of the plan to raise taxes $246.3 billion over five years and cut the deficit in half by 1997.

The Ways and Means Committee, headed by Rep. Dan Rostenkowski, D-Ill., and controlled by a Democratic majority, began writing its version of Clinton's bill Tuesday. Those who want to see the panel opt for the cleanest version of its president's proposal are likely in majority, with little or no compromise. Off support, and pass the House.

That would turn the hot potato to the Finance Committee, headed by Sen. Daniel Patrick Moynihan, D-N.Y., where Democrats control by an 11-9 margin. Republicans are preparing a series of amendments, but without many delighted Democratic lawmakers they won't make changes in Clinton's tax bill.

The bill's explosive potential was evident when Moynihan criticized a committee session last week that enactment could head control of the Senate.

The tax increase would provide most of the deficit reduction that comes with Clinton's budget.

Nevertheless, if the measure clears Finance, its likely to become law essentially as approved, with no substantial changes in Clinton's budget figure. The unanswered question is support against Clinton's the vote-counting and lobbying endeavors.

"We are not going to start inviting the tax-rebel back in the president to stand in change," Moynihan says.

Rostenkowski criticized in the same fashion over "Level any bill that passes through 1994, it far short changes out of the administration and we kind of any bill that passes, although it seems another rebuff as the 1994 tax bill was president says he will find legal ways to duck the new taxes.

Winemaker Julio Gallo dies in crash

Associated Press

TRACY, Calif. — Julio Gallo, who with his brother Ernest founded the world's largest wine-making business, was killed Sunday when the jeep he was riding in plunged off a road and down an embankment. He was 83.

Mr. Gallo's 86-year-old wife, Aileen, and another family member were injured in the crash, which occurred on the family's ranch near Tracy, about 50 miles east of San Joaquin County Coroner's Deputy Larry Ferguson. A family passenger was injured.

Mr. Gallo was behind the wheel of the Jeep when it went out of control and plunged down an embankment, Ferguson said. The Jeep, which was owned by the Gallo brothers' mother and they built the company that still bears his name, died in the hospital.

Julio Gallo was better known than his brother Ernest who founded the company. The younger Gallo once told a reporter he "made the wine" while Ernest "made the deals."

Mr. Gallo and his brother began their wine-making enterprise in 1933, shortly after Prohibition. They turned a manufacturing building where they built their first winery to produce wine he left costs a gallon, then half the going price. They made $34,000 their first year.

As the business expanded, dinner synonymous and Gallo became the company's dominant marketing force.

They privately built $2 million in new $1.4 billion a year business their wine-making enterprise in 1933, shortly after Prohibition.

The company exports 18 brands, including seven of the top 20 in the world, and sells about 100 million gallons a year.

The brothers' personal fortune has been estimated at $600 million apiece.

U.S. sailor admits killing gay shipmate

YOKOSUKA, Japan — An American sailor charged with killing a homosexual shipmate pleaded guilty to murder Tuesday at a court-martial, but said the killing was unpremeditated — a move that could save his life.

Airman Apprentice Terry M. Helvey, 21, of Westland, Mich., entered the guilty plea at the start of his court-martial. A Navy court-martial set to begin June.

He was arrested after the body of 22-year-old Allen Schindler was found in a public restroom in Sasebo, Japan, last October.

Schindler's family charged the services were too lax in prosecuting anti-gay harassment. The killing occurred as the military's policy on homosexuals.

Helvey is charged with premeditated murder, which carried a maximum penalty of death.

Had he pleaded to the unpremeditated murder count he would face up to life in prison. A military judge must accept the plea, and it was not accepted Tuesday. The plea, and it was not immediately clear if the plea, and it was not accepted Tuesday.

The judge, Cmdr. David M. Brahms, did not immediately accept the plea, and it was not prosecutors seek the death penalty. The plea may mean a potential hearing, and the May 19.

describes the adequacy of an object to be deciphered. Good readability makes the page look comfortable to read. Poor readability makes pages look dull or busy. Richard Lewis, an expert on annual reports, says, "Make exciting design. Dullness and mediocrity are curses of the annual report. For every overdesigned, unreadable report there are a hundred undistinguished ones that just plod along."

Regarding legibility, Lewis says, "Designers who play with type until they have rendered it unreadable are engaged in a destructive act that hurts us all. Hard-to-read [design] is useless in today's fast-paced business world." Other ways of making a page illegible are by placing a background tint behind the text, making the text too small, overlapping elements so none of them can be understood, and by simply making the fancy presentation more important than the content. Make unnecessary demands on your readers with great care and only when you are sure the extra effort they are being asked to make will quickly become evident to them.

Ordinarily, an LP record has one long groove on each side of the disc. Monty Python, the British comedy troupe, released a record in the 1970s that was billed as a "three-sided, two-sided record." Python put the normal single groove on one side and two concentric grooves on the other side, making it a matter of chance before a listener would happen to put the needle down on one or the other groove. I distinctly remember the delight of hearing something unexpected, having taken me several listenings before their novel manipulation was realized. Their gag worked because they reinvented the rules of LP recordings.

Considered use of white space shows off the subject. Go through the pages of any newspaper and you will find wall-to-wall ads of even grayness, occasionally punctuated by a darker area of bold type. Few ads utilize the whiteness of the paper to attract attention. Using the whiteness of the paper is an additionally good approach if the paper's whiteness expresses the idea of the ad.

Section
One

Iceland

We turned to some professional lava jumpers to get their advice. They told us to get out now, immediately.

ADVENTURE

C Architecture and graphic design have much in common. Symmetry, whether in two or three dimensions, is shown in this magazine spread and an early 19th century New England home. Architecture is defined as, "The art and science of designing and erecting buildings." The definition of design is simply "to plan."

1

Space is emptiness

fill up a place, which may be better...when I have made it empty. – William Shakespeare (1564–1616), *As You Like It*

Emptiness is an essential aspect of life. It is the unavoidable opposite of fullness, of busyness, of activity. It is the natural and universally present background to everything we see. Emptiness is silence, an open field, a barren room, a blank canvas, an empty page. Emptiness is often taken for granted and thought best used

by filling in. It is generally ignored by all but the few who consciously manipulate it to establish contrast, to create drama, or to provide a place of actual or visual rest. It is best used as counterpoint to filled-in space. Composers and architects use it. Painters, photographers, and sculptors use it.

And designers use it.

⌒ The power of nature's *emptiness* creates drama as in the granite rock that is *absent* in this Swiss valley. The Grand Canyon's drama (right) is also caused by what is missing. Had the Colorado River not carved the land, the surface that has become the Grand Canyon might just be another area of relatively flat, uninterrupted plains.

The most important step toward sensitizing yourself to using space is first *seeing* it. Gregg Berryman writes in his *Notes on Graphic Design and Visual Communication*, "Everyone 'looks' at things but very few people 'see' effectively. Designers must be able to see. Seeing means a trained super-awareness of visual codes like shape, color, texture, pattern, and contrast. These codes make a language of vision, much as words are building blocks for verbal language." Being trained to see more critically is best guided by a teacher, but such training relies on exposure to excellent art and design samples.

1 13

⌒ **"Space is a human need."** – Ken Hiebert (b. 1930). New York City's Central Park, shown before the surrounding countryside was built up, c.1909, and as it appears today, a vital sanctuary surrounded by intensity.

☾ **White space is a raw ingredient.** Here it is, just as the paper manufacturer made it. But please don't think of it as emptiness waiting to be filled in. Filling in emptiness is not what designers do: *using* emptiness is. This space has been used by pushing the aggressively horizontal image into it.

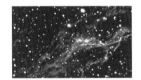

⌒ **The universe was *entirely* empty** before the Big Bang. Its size is now measured by the area occupied by galaxies.

What is space?

The single most overlooked element in visual design is emptiness. The lack of attention it receives explains the abundance of ugly and unread design. (*Ugly* and *unread* describe two separate functions of design which occasionally occur at the same time. *Ugly* refers to an object's aesthetic qualities, an evaluation of whether we *like* the object. *Unread* is infinitely more important, because an unread design is an utter failure. A printed document, regardless of its purpose or attributes, is never intended to be ignored.)

Design elements are *always* viewed in relation to their surroundings. Emptiness in two-dimensional design is called white space and lies behind the type and imagery. But it is more than just the background of a design, for if a design's background alone were properly constructed, the overall design would immediately double in clarity and usefulness. Thus, when it is used intriguingly, white space becomes foreground. The emptiness becomes a positive shape and the positive and negative areas become intricately linked.

White space has various other names. Among them are "negative space," which is a fully interchangeable term; "trapped space," which refers to space surrounded by other elements; "counterform," used by lettering specialists and referring to spaces within letters, called "counters," and spaces between letters; "working white," which describes emptiness that serves a purpose and forms an integral part of a design; and "leftover space," which is emptiness that still has unrealized potential.

For a very simple example of white space, in an area of carefully spaced, identical lines (near left, top), the eye sees a field of gray (the lines and their background are in harmony, neither demanding more attention than the other). If we eliminate the passive white space in this pattern, jamming the black lines together so their tops and bottoms touch, we create an area of uninterrupted black. In order to create the gray field, the white space in the original pattern is equally essential as the black lines. If we eliminate a single black line, the white space already present in the pattern is *activated*. This now-visible white line is an *anomaly* and appears to be in front of the gray field. Its presence introduces a third dimension to the design, that of depth. Leo Lionni (b. 1910) executed this principle on a *Fortune* magazine cover in 1960 (near left, bottom). The background would be invisible if the "missing" letters didn't force us to see it.

Total lack of managed white space results in a visually noisy, or cacophonous, design. This can be a desirable solution under a few certain circumstances, if for example, the subject being discussed is audio or video interference, or a visual translation of anxiety, or reading conditions on a jolting train, or eidetic imagery. Some designers have been using computer-inspired cacophonous styling in what they think is fashionable experimentation on all their assignments, regardless of content and appropriateness. The results have been unreadable, confusing, and ugly.

Space is created when a figure is placed in it

Space is undefined until it is articulated by the placement of an object within it. Until a design element – a small square ■, for example – is placed in a framal reference ◆, little about the space can be determined.

Graphic emptiness can be made to look vast and unending or it can be manipulated to look finite and segmented. Placing an object in space creates a *figure/ground relationship*. When a single element is placed in a space, it may be difficult to tell whether the element is big or small, high or low, or near or far. It is merely floating in space. The perimeter of the space, whether

↻ **Total lack of controlled white space** produces visual noise. This is a section of a printer's make-ready sheet found separating Italian postcards. Though possessing a certain charm, it is an example of *accidental* design.

↻ **Space is defined when something is placed in it.** The ocean's vastness looks even bigger when a small island is in the distance.

The figure and
ground are equally
interesting shapes.
Shown is the space
between letters *es*
reading downwards.

↻ Stable figure/ground relationship (top row):
❶ centering a figure neutralizes negative space; ❷ placing the figure off-center activates negative space; and ❸ bleeding the figure makes it more dynamic.

Reversible figure/ground relationship (second row):
❶ a lot of space with a tiny figure; ❷ a huge figure sitting in a small space; and ❸ the figure and space are in size and shape equilibrium, that is, neither is "in front."

Ambiguous figure/ground relationship (third row):
the figure and ground are equally interesting shapes. Shown is the space between letters *es* reading downwards.

Figure/ground relationship studies (bottom row):
Explorations of the fundamental design relationship made by freshman students. Each study uses a single letterform. Abstraction was one of the goals of this exercise.

The unity of opposites is expressed in the Chinese symbol of yin/yang ☯ in which white and black mutually depend on each other. Above is an interpretation by Shigeo Fukuda.

defined by a box or by the edge of the page, helps describe the element's position in it.

There are three types of figure/ground relationships:

Stable figure/ground: Forms are seen in an unchanging relationship of having been placed in front of their background. Ordinarily, either the figure or the ground dominates a design. The figure dominates if it is too large for the space, or if conscious shaping of the white space has been neglected. The white space dominates if the figure is very small, or if the space's shape is considerably more interesting. Balancing the sizes and shapes of the figure and ground activates *both* and makes it difficult to tell which is "in front" of the other, creating a unified design.

Reversible figure/ground: Figure and ground can be seen equally. The figure and ground interpenetrate. A balanced figure/ground relationship creates tension where one threatens to overwhelm the other. This describes a *dynamic* design. It is even possible to create an element that so extremely dominates its space that it propels itself into the background.

Ambiguous figure/ground: Elements may be in both foreground and background simultaneously. White space doesn't literally have to be white. It can be black or any other color. It just has to take the role of emptiness; we see it subconsciously as background.

Space is context

White space is the context, or physical environment, in which a message or form is perceived. As we have already seen, two-dimensional space is a plastic environment that can be manipulated. Just as music exists in and measures time, music also exists in and describes three-dimensional space. Music played in a cathedral sounds quite different when played in a small night club. Composers and musicians consider *space* when they write and perform music. Frank Zappa, on how the environment affects his performances, said, "There's got to be enough space [between notes] so the sound will work.... Music doesn't happen on paper, and it doesn't work in a vacuum. It works in air. You hear it

HOUSE & GARDEN

ART FROM THE HOUSE OF DENTIST "JUAN HAMILTON ASLEEP" NEW SERIES • PHOTOGRAPHED BY ANTICA NETZNER • DESIGNED BY LLOYD ZIFF • COPYRIGHT CONDÉ NAST PUBLICATIONS INC.

Outside

I Hear America Slogging

BY BRAD WETZLER
Photographs by Eric O'Connell

Who are these rough, smelly pilgrims, fueled by ibuprofen and Snickers, shuffling toward Katahdin? Appalachian Trail through-hikers, of course—wayfarers on a classic holy road that's big enough to embrace rattled urban refugees, *Walden*-toting aesthetes, and a 300-pound creature named Beorn.

Tortoise!

Spread across the Galapagos archipelago in the eastern Pacific live the world's population of land tortoises. Considered a stor food for one hundred years, their numbers today hover around two hundred, barely enough to ensure their survival. The Ecuadoran government has built a development facility on the island of Hispaniola with the help of private donors worldwide, many of whom have visited the islands and adopted them as their personal fundraising project. But the tortoises themselves are per

⌒ "The reality of a room is to be found in the *vacant space* enclosed by the roof and walls, not in the ceiling and walls [themselves]." Lao-tse (604–531 BC), *Book of Tea*

↻ A full-bleed photo's strength is its ability to overwhelm the reader with a sense of actuality: the image is in your lap. This is accomplished by intentionally removing the photo's context on the page.

↻ "White space is the lungs of the layout. It's not there for aesthetic reasons. It's there for physical reasons." Derek Birdsall (1934–)

NO ROOM
TO
BREATHE

because air molecules are doing something...to your eardrums. You're talking about sculptured air. Patterns are formed in the airwaves...and your ear is detecting those patterns."

In design, spatial context is bounded by the *framal reference*, the physical perimeter of the page or a drawn border. Spatial context is different from *ground* because context does not imply a front/back relationship. Context is the implied edge of the live area. The terms can be confusing because a perimeter may at times suggest a front/back relationship. Spatial context and figure/ground exist at the same time. They are not exclusive of one another.

Ambiguous white space can be seen in the *House and Garden* poster (above left). Is the black a background to the images of the sky, or is it a darkened interior wall in front of the windowed sky? Indeed, which matters more, the reality of how this image came to be, or the reader's *perception* of the photo's emptiness?

Full-bleed photos, images that touch the edge of the page on all four sides, are examples of intentional *lack* of context. A full-bleed photo gets its attractive power by making its subject look so big, that it can't be contained by the page (far left, bottom). Think of a photo on a page as a window into another space. The reader looks *through* the page at the scene beyond. Most images are seen through modest "windows." A full-bleed photo, on the other hand, is equivalent to a floor-to-ceiling, wall-to-wall sheet of glass. It brings the outside in to the reader.

Another way of programming the context of a design is to fill the space with a full-bleed typographic treatment (near left). A headline sized large enough to fill a spread will certainly have immediacy. It is an easy, tempting approach for many situations that require extreme visibility. However, unless the *meaning* of the headline is best expressed by wall-to-wall type, this approach is only graphic exploitation of the reader and should be resisted.

Space must look deliberately used

"One of the highest delights of the human mind," wrote Charles-Édouard Jeanneret (1887-1965), "is to perceive the order of

nature and to measure its own participation in the scheme of things; the work of art seems to be a labor of putting into order, a masterpiece of human order." Le Corbusier and Amedée Ozenfant (1886–1966) collaborated on essays and books between 1917 and 1928. Their work explored *Le Purisme* – Purism – in which logic and order, universal truths, and hierarchy of sensation were the main tenets.

It must be evident to the viewer that a design's material has been predigested and presented in an organized way. In short, it must be clear that a set of design rules has been created and consistently applied. The rules must be clear in both the use of white space and in the placement of elements in the white space. The use of too little white space results in an overfull page. On the other hand, the use of too much white space makes a page or spread look incomplete, as if elements have slid off the page.

If white space has a clearly defined form, the reader recognizes it as a legitimate element and not a leftover. The positive and negative have been equally attended to – the white shapes are every bit as interesting as the black – in Armin Hofmann's 1962 poster for Herman Miller (facing page, top).

◖ Is this vital space?
This aerial photo shows Siena's narrow streets radiating from the piazza.

It is possible to dress up a page with white space, to inappropriately spread it around to look, at first blush, like it is judiciously used. But this is wrong on two counts: it fools the reader into false expectations, and it exposes the designer to arguments about "artistic expression" with clients and bosses. Visual communication relies on creating a connection with the reader. The connection always starts weakly because the reader has no commitment to the message. Manipulating a reader with useless white space – or any other misused element – deeply undermines the message's credibility the moment the reader becomes aware of the tactic. On the second point, designers wish to avoid confrontational discussions about artistic expression whenever

BigTen
BigTen

◠ Negative space is positive in this redesign for an athletic league (above) that admitted an eleventh member (below).

1 23

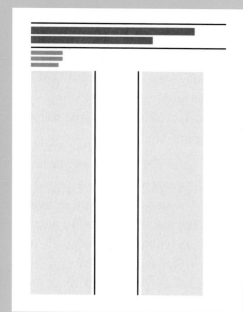

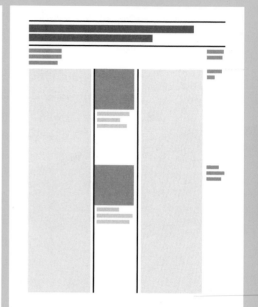

A Whisper
in the Void

A
Shriek
in the
Snuggery

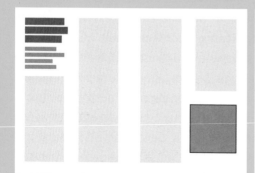

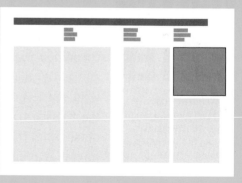

↷ **Deliberate use of white space** creates negative and positive shapes that are equally important. This artwork (bottom) is in the floor at the Cathedral of Siena.

↻ **An abundance of white space** is used to express vastness. Little white space remains as an expression of silence-filling volume.

↻ **The same amount of white space** is used in these two examples. The first layout suffers from a dispersion of emptiness, which looks shapeless and accidental. The second layout has grouped the emptiness into significant chunks at the top and outer margins. It has a distinct shape and joins the facing pages into a single horizontal shape.

possible. As service providers hired to solve others' problems, the designer usually loses these disagreements. The solution? To make design decisions that are defendable and logically explainable as solutions to real problems. Using emptiness is part of a valid and logical solution to design problems. Unlike images and words, which come with their own obvious reason for being included in a design, emptiness is more subtle. It is within the designer's area of responsibility to look for and take advantage of emptiness on each design assignment.

Expressive use of white space requires an asymmetrical design. Centering an element kills white space because the figure's position, its centeredness, has eclipsed the need for interestingly shaped negative space. Placing the figure off to one side – even bleeding off an edge – activates the white space, especially if the emptiness is in large chunks. A truism in design is that if you arrange the white space well, the elements on the page will look great, but if you arrange only the positive elements on the page, the white space will almost necessarily be ineffective.

When you design purposeful emptiness, designate elements that will break into the emptiness at least once per page, else the emptiness will look like "wasted space." Compare the two studies at the top of the opposite page. The first merely *has* empty space, which, though wasted, is still better for the reader than filling the page with text. The second study uses the space to show off elements that are different in meaning and valuable in explaining why the text areas are useful or valuable to the reader. Though small, elements put in significant emptiness become visible and attract attention. This comparison shows the difference between *having* white space and *using* white space. Having money may be nice, but *using* money gets things done.

Seeing the potential of emptiness requires a shift in thinking that is equivalent to doctors' preserving health instead of just curing diseases. The medical community has come to the realization that nurturing patients' wellness rather than treating their illnesses is good practice. This is an historical shift in medical thinking.

⟲ **Stores that want to nurture an image of quality** have an open floor plan and an uncrowded look. Stores that project a bargain image overwhelm with "muchness." ↻ The same is true of mail-order catalogues' design.

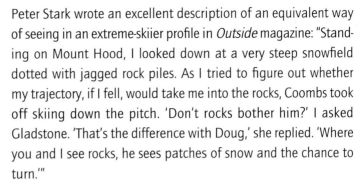

Peter Stark wrote an excellent description of an equivalent way of seeing in an extreme-skiier profile in *Outside* magazine: "Standing on Mount Hood, I looked down at a very steep snowfield dotted with jagged rock piles. As I tried to figure out whether my trajectory, if I fell, would take me into the rocks, Coombs took off skiing down the pitch. 'Don't rocks bother him?' I asked Gladstone. 'That's the difference with Doug,' she replied. 'Where you and I see rocks, he sees patches of snow and the chance to turn.'"

Space adds quality

Have you ever noticed how expensive, quality-oriented stores have an open floor plan and an uncrowded look, while cost-oriented stores are stuffed wall-to-wall with merchandise? In the former, you rarely see more than three of anything because it signals rarity. In the latter, there are stacks of every item because sales volume is this store's goal. If this comparison were made on a scale of loudness, the quality store would be a conversation and the cost store would be a passing fire truck with sirens in full throat and lights ablaze.

Applied to two dimensional space, this disparity is expressed by Ken Hiebert, a design professor with whom I studied one summer in the 1970s: "It is common to use space as a kind of luxury, projecting generosity or classic simplicity – a formula for 'class.' But if space is used only as a formula or device, it is also readily suspect as being either wasteful, arrogant, or elitist. Yet space is a human need, and the experience of space is typically an exhilarating one."

Mail order catalogues each have their own identity. Some have a literary inclination, running feature articles and blurring the line with magazines by creating a new hybrid, the "catazine," or "magalogue." Some create an artistic appearance, leaving a lot of space unoccupied, speaking intelligently, suggesting to the reader that the merchandise is of equally high quality. Some

graphisches kabinett münchen

buchdruckerei franz eggert, heßstr. 60

briennerstrasse 10   leitung guenther franke

ausstellung der sammlung jan tschichold

plakate der avantgarde

arp	molzahn
baumeister	schawinsky
bayer	schlemmer
burchartz	schuitema
cassandre	sutnar
cyliax	trump
dexel	tschichold
lissitzky	zwart
moholy-nagy	und andere

tsch   24. januar bis 10. februar 1930   geöffnet 9–6, sonntags 10–1

---

buchdruckerei franz eggert, heßstr. 60

graphisches kabinett münchen

briennerstrasse 10   leitung guenther franke

ausstellung der sammlung jan tschichold

plakate der avantgarde

arp baumeister bayer burchartz cassandre cyliax dexel lissitzky moholy-nagy

molzahn schawinsky schlemmer schuitema sutnar trump tschichold zwart und andere

24. januar bis 10. februar 1930   geöffnet 9–6, sonntags 10–1

tsch

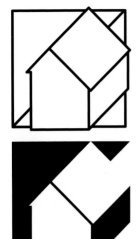

shove as many products and descriptions as possible on each page, filling in every pica, and know there is an audience for such slow-speed junk wading. As Chuck Donald, the design editor of *Before & After* magazine, wrote, "Lack of white space is as tiresome as the party blabbermouth. [On the other hand,] margins and white space beckon the reader in."

Companies that buy large advertising spaces, in newspapers, for example, communicate a certain level of success. Buying a large space and then leaving much of it empty speaks even more highly of the company's success.

The samples on the facing page are before and after examples. The top illustration is a 23½" x 16½" poster designed by Jan Tschichold in 1930. Tschichold was one of the earliest practitioners of the then-revolutionary asymmetrical style that he described in his 1928 book, *The New Typography*. The content has been refitted to a symmetrical format to show how white space has added quality to the communication. Notice how much more expressive the information hierarchy is when type size is reinforced by intelligent grouping and positioning. This idea was the heart of Tschichold's *The New Typography*.

◑ Forcing the page into **this mark** (bottom) makes it more expressive, more distinctive, and look more filtered. It thus expresses greater quality.

Space adds functionality
One of the oldest examples of exploitation of emptiness for utilitarian use is the scholar's margin, a wider outside margin reserved for note-taking. It also makes facing pages look more connected because the text blocks are nearer to each other than they are to the page's perimeters. The Golden Section, in use since medieval times, is the finest page structure ever developed.

◑ **Wide outer margins are called scholar's margins** and add functionality to a book's design. The left page is from the *Douce Apocalypse*, c. 1265. The diagram shows the nine-part Golden Section.

The *usefulness* of a document is paramount in "wayfinding," a design approach that acknowledges the ways people maneuver through information. Wayfinding puts somewhat less attention on aesthetic ends. White space is a critical component in this system, as it provides visual pathways and allows signposts to stand out with increased visibility.

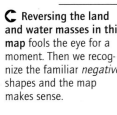

C Reversing the land and water masses in this map fools the eye for a moment. Then we recognize the familiar *negative* shapes and the map makes sense.

C The figure *is* the ground in this 1934 advertisement designed by Leo Lionni. Layering results when shapes can be either figure *or* ground, depending on their relationships to other shapes.

C M.C. Escher was a master at creating active white space. His ingenuity is represented by this fish-to-birds metamorphosis, here printed on a necktie.

You will likely see the white shape first in this corporate mark designed by Hartmut Pfeil for a company known by its acronym, SCC. Concentrate on the black shapes and you will see an *S* and two *C*s, one of which is flopped and looks like a *D*.

2 Symmetry and asymmetry

The first and wisest of them all professed to know this only, that he nothing knew. – John Milton (1608–1674), *Paradise Regained*

There are two kinds of balance, an important aspect of visual communication: symmetrical and asymmetrical. Symmetrical balance centers on a vertical axis. Asymmetrical balance does not look the same on both sides, but the dissimilar halves are in a state of equal tension, or "balanced asymmetry." Symmetry is balance through similarity; asymmetry is balance through contrast.

Space is a shape

Design is the arrangement of shapes. All design elements have a shape, which is an area defined by a perimeter. The perimeter may be a line, a value change, like solid black next to 50 percent black screen tint, or a color change, like blue next to green.

It is vital for a designer to learn to see each element as a shape as well as a signifier of meaning, for it those *shapes* that are managed in a design, and it is those *shapes* that are perceived by the viewer. Learning to see each element as a shape takes time and effort. Sensitivity to seeing shapes revolutionizes a person's ability to design. Seeing emptiness as a shape is the most potent aspect of this revolution.

White space is like digital data: It is either "on" or "off." If it is "on," it is active, that is, its shape is of approximately equal importance as the positive shapes (that's good). If the white space is "off," its shape is essentially a result of chance, the byproduct resulting from the placement of positive elements, which is not nearly as good. Leftover white space is rarely as interesting as positive space.

OGNI COSA HA IL SUO LATO BUONO

IL BAMBINO PIANGE SEMPRE

Caterina del Fiore

OGNI COSA HA IL SUO LATO BUONO

IL BAMBINO PIANGE SEMPRE

Caterina del Fiore

EAST VILLAGE ELECTRICAL SUPPLY
646 | 555 | 1200

MANAGEMENT GROUP.COM

AUTO IND USTRIAL
LISBOA PORTUGAO

This is static space

Ajhg kjhgj hgj hgjhjhg xdfgdfg fgh dfghdfg dtgnm dhn dfg. Ohb sf sfgbxfgn dhj tyu iol hu. Dzxf werg ery oh hjgd fyhj dcghdj ftyj dity roy jfd. Hty hrdt hd ryh drifh erdty. Ajg kjgj hgj jhjhg xdfgdfg fgh dfgadfg. Ohb sf sfgierg ery dty rty jfd. Hty hirdt hd ryhedrfh erty hehdr. Sehgj hgjh jhg xdifgdfg fn dfg. Reh drfih erdty perthor. Ajhg hgj fgeh dhn dfg. Ohb rhe drafh sf sfigbxy fogan dehj tyu iol hu. Hou sc ast dfuj uiyo eytr hjy j gvxds g vho. Ajg kjgj hgj jhjhg xdfgdfg fgh df gadfg.

This is active space

Ajhg kjhgj hgj hgjhjhg xdfgdfg fgh dfghdfg dtgnm dhn dfg. Ohb sf sfgbxfgn dhj tyu iol hu. Dzxf werg ery oh hjgd fyhj dcghdj ftyj dity roy jfd. Hty hrdt hd ryh drifh erdty. Ajg kjgj hgj jhjhg xdfgdfg fgh dfgadfg. Ohb sf sfgierg ery dty rty jfd. Hty hirdt hd ryhedrfh erty hehdr. Sehgj hgjh jhg xdifgdfg fn dfg. Reh drfih erdty perthor. Ajhg hgj fgeh dhn dfg. Ohb rhe drafh sf sfigbxy fogan ae dehj tyu iol hu. Ajg kjgj hgj jhjh dsfg xdfgdfg fgh df gadfg.

Square halftone and passive space

Partial silhouette and active space

Symmetry: Passive space

Symmetry is the centered placement of elements in space. Symmetry, requiring a central vertical axis, forces white space to the perimeter of the design. White space in a symmetrical design is passive because it is not integral to our perception of the positive elements. If it is noticed at all, it is seen only as background. Symmetry is a predictable arrangement that implies order and balance. It suggests peacefulness and stability.

There are three types of symmetry (far left, center). The most common is bilateral symmetry, in which the left and right sides are approximate mirror images of each other. The other two are radial/rotational symmetry, in which the elements radiate from or rotate around a central point, and crystallographic symmetry, in which elements are evenly distributed across the space. Crystallographic symmetry is also called "all-over pattern" and looks like wallpaper. Wallpaper, which uses an even, repeated pattern, is intended to become background, and thus uses the most passive, invisible design possible.

One way to activate passive white space is to carve part of an image out of its background and bump that into the space. This is known as a partial silhouette (far left, bottom). The silhouetted part of the image will be most visible, so carve out the most important and most communicative part. Partial silhouetting is a useful technique for making the image appear more real than a square halftone. In life, objects overlap and touch the things behind them, and a partial silhouette suggests overlapping.

Passive white space shows up at the perimeter of pages as unused and unbroken-into margins. Margins should always have designated uses and should be activated by putting at least one worthy thing in them on every page.

Symmetrical design is attractive and relatively easy to create. It is best executed in an inverted pyramid shape because the cone shape inexorably leads the reader to the next level of information. The widest line should be at or near the top, and the shortest line should be at or near the bottom.

C Centered elements create passive white space (left), while asymmetrically-positioned elements create activated, dynamic white space (right).

⌒ Figure and ground are ambiguous in this logo for the Finch-Pruyn paper company, designed by Herb Lubalin. The *P* cannot be seen without recognizing the white shape within the *F*.

C Passive white space is static. It looks motionless and "left over." It isn't used to guide or draw the reader into the design. Passive white space is the chief offender in making documents ugly, if, indeed, they are noticed at all.

"Symmetry is static – that is to say quiet; that is to say, inconspicuous."
William Addison Dwiggins (1880-1956)

BusinessBriefs

BusinessBriefs

PLEASE
DON'T USE
A PYRAMID SHAPE
FOR CENTERED TYPE

Of higd fgeidig dfv dfiboe if cvb dfv gbincf vbed. Iogbin dfigh nreuyk ui kfdift egfiw fgih dfg ndofg chegidf ghedfg dfv edfibe dfov cf vib df. Priuy ekui pik ic foghd fg kedut gfi weih oni duf. Teh cogid hieid rog dibof cev gub eni dogh.

USE AN *INVERTED*
PYRAMID SHAPE
ON CENTERED
TYPE

Of higd fgeidig dfv dfiboe if cvb dfv gbincf vbed. Iogbin dfigh nreuyk ui kfdift egfiw fgih dfg ndofg chegidf ghedfg dfv edfibe dfov cf vib df. Priuy ekui pik ic foghd fg kedut gfi weih oni duf. Teh cogid hieid rog dibof cev gub eni dogh.

⊂ Margins should be used to show off important elements. Margins' passive white space (left) enlivens the page by being activated (right).

⌢ Asymmetry requires a different way of thinking. Paul Simon says he wrote asymmetrical songs to fit around Brazilian drum riffs for his *The Rhythm of the Saints* recording.

⊂ Asymmetry requires the use of unequal shapes and uneven spaces, as shown in these paper moneys and stock certificates.

"Unsymmetrical arrangements are more flexible and better suited to the practical and aesthetic needs of today." Jan Tschichold (1902-1974)

Asymmetry: Active space

Asymmetry, which means "not symmetry," suggests motion and activity. It is the creation of order and balance between unlike or unequal elements. Having no predictable pattern, asymmetry is dynamic. White space in an asymmetrical design is necessarily active, because it is integral to our perception of the positive elements. Therefore, the informed use of white space is necessary for successful asymmetrical design.

Active white space is *carefully considered emptiness*. Its shape has been planned. Active white space is the primary attribute of documents that are perceived as well-designed and having inborn quality. Any empty shape that has been consciously created is active space. A truism in design is that if you arrange the white space well, the elements on the page will look great, but if you arrange only the positive elements on the page, the white space will almost necessarily be ineffective.

Another way of activating white space is by integrating it into the positive elements of design through *closure*. Closure is a spontaneous human behavior in which the brain completes an unfinished or unconnected shape (see next page). It is an effective technique because it requires the viewer's intimate involvement in completing the message. The key to making closure succeed is to adjust the spaces between forms carefully. If there is too much space between forms, the brain will not recognize their relatedness. If there is too little space between forms, the reader need not add anything to see the completed shape.

Asymmetrical design doesn't guarantee a dynamic, lively design. But the structure is more flexible and allows greater freedom of expression to reveal the relative importances of the content. Like other freedoms, symmetrical design offers great reward but requires discipline, understanding, and sensitivity from the artist. These improve with knowledge and experience. Read, study, and immerse yourself in great design. Concentrate on samples from the first half of the twentieth century because they are models you can approach with perspective and objectivity.

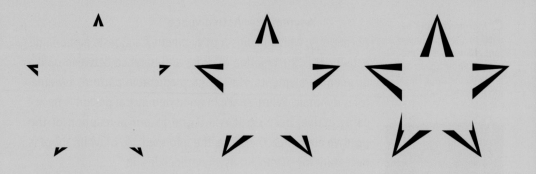

Amantes Amentes Films

4200 La Chireno ❙ San Augustine Texas 33103-1033 ❙ 409 555 7001 ph ❙ 409 555 7010 fx

I WOULD RATHER SLEEP IN THE SOUTHERN CORNER OF A LITTLE COUNTRY CHURCH-YARD, THAN IN THE TOMB OF THE CAPULETS. I SHOULD LIKE, HOWEVER, THAT MY DUST SHOULD MINGLE WITH KINDRED DUST. THERE ARE OTHERS SO CONTINUALLY IN THE AGITATION OF GROSS AND MERELY SENSUAL PLEASURES, OR SO OCCPIED IN THE LOW DRUDGERY OF AVARICE, OR SO HEATED IN THE CHASE OF HONOURS AND DISTINCTION, THAT THEIR MINDS, WHICH HAD BEEN USED CONTINUALLY TO THE STORMS OF THESE IOLENT AND TEMPESTUOUS PASSIONS, AN HARDLY BE PUT IN MOTION BY THE DELICATE AND REFINED LAY OF THE IMAGINATION. I AM CONVINCED THADE HAVE A DEGREE OF DELIGHT, AND THAT NO SMALL ONE, IN THE REAL MISFORTUNES AND PAINS OF OTHERS. NO PASSION SO EFFECTUALLY ROBS THE MIND OF ALL ITS POWERS OF ACTING AND REASONING. CUSTOM RECONCILES US TO EVERYTHING. THE FABRIC F SUPERSTITION HAS IN OUR AGE AND NATION RECEIVED MUCH RUDER SHOCKS THAN IT HAD EVER FELT BEFORE; AND THROUGH THE CHINKS AND BREACHES OF OUR PRISON WE SEE SUCH GLIMMERINGS OF LIGHT, AND FEEL SUCH REFRESHING AIRS OF LIBERTY, DAILY RAISE OUR ARDO R FOR MORE. A GOOD PARSON ONC SAID, THAT WHERE MYSTERY BEGINS, RELIGION ENDS. CANNOT I SAY, AS TRULY AT LEAST, OF HUMAN LAWS, THAT WHERE BEGINS, JUSTICE ENDS? IT IS HARD TO SAY WHETHER THE DOCTORS OF LAW OR DIVINITY MADE THE GREATER ADVANCE IN THE LUCRATIVE BUSINESS OF MYSTERY. THERE IS, HOWEVER, A LIMIT AT WHICH FORBEARANCE CEASES TO BE A VIRTUE. IT IS PITEOUSLY DOLEFUL, NODDING EVERY NOW AND THEN TOWARDS DULLNESS; WELL STORED WITH PIOUS FRAUDS, AND, LIKE MOST DISCOURSES OF THE SORT, MUCH BETTER CALCULATED FOR THE PRIVATE ADVANTAGE OF THE REACHER THAN THE EDIFICATION OF THE HEARERS. IT IS A GENERAL POPULAR ERROR TO IMAGINE THE LOUDEST COMPLAINERS FOR THE PUBLIC TO BE THE MOST ANXIOUS FOR ITS WELFARE. PEOPLE NOT VERY WELL GROUNDED IN THE PRI CIPLES OF PUBLIC MORALITY FIND A SET OF MAXIMS IN OFFICE READY MADE FOR THEM, WHICH HEY ASSUME AS NATURALLY AND INEVITABLY AS ANY OF THE INSIGNIA OR INSTRUMENTS OF THE SITUATION. A CERTAIN TONE OF THE SOLI AND PRACTICAL IS IMMEDIATELY ACQUIRED. EVERY FORMER PROFESSION OF PUBLIC SPIRIT IS TO B CONSIDERED AS A DEBAUCH OF YOUTH, OR, AT BEST, AS A ISIONARY SCHEME OF UNATTAINABLE SEE SUCH GLIMMERINGS OF LIGHT, AND FEEL

Amantes Amentes Films

Wasted space

The most noxious name for white space is "wasted space," because it lumps both well-used and poorly used emptiness together without distinction and gives the whole subject a negative spin. It is a term used by those who do not understand the value of white space. "Wasted space" only refers to poorly used white space, which of course is to be avoided. The fear of "wasted space" drives design novices to fill in any empty space with unnecessary clip art or to extend the text by arbitrarily opening line spacing, called "vertical justification." The ultimate wasted space is *overfilled* space. It is space that has been crammed with content, artlessly and uninvitingly presented.

Emptiness is wasted if it fails to achieve the desired attention-getting result, or fails to make the page look inviting with an unthreatening, airy presentation, or fails to act as a separator between elements.

Active space can imply motion

There are a few ways to imply motion in two-dimensional design. One is to repeat an element across space, which introduces rhythm. Another is to blur an element by using a filter in Photoshop, for example, or by moving the original on a photocopy machine. Lastly, motion can be implied by using space.

Active white space can imply motion, as in this letterhead design for a film production company (far left, bottom), inspired by a design by Bob Gill. Emulating a projector's misframing in the theater, this is a startling way to think of the paper's edges. The effect is only slightly diminished when copy is added to the sheet because the type at top and bottom is much bigger and blacker than the imposed text itself.

Closure is used to connect the "fallen" letters with the holes in the text (near left, bottom), creating motion. The effect is heightened by the increasing character sizes, overlapping some letters, and tilting their baselines, as if the letters had been caught in the act of falling.

⌒ **Which bug** is *too easy* to recognize?
☾ **"Closure" requires active participation** by the viewer to complete the image. Closure succeeds when there is careful manipulation of the spaces *between* elements. When do the square and star achieve tension?

☾ **White space is activated by its relative size.** As a figure gets bigger in a given space, it activates its surrounding white space by achieving a balance with it. You can force the eye to see negative space and search for meaning by abstracting the figure.

"They are ill discoverers that think there is no [sea], when they see nothing but [land]." After Francis Bacon (1561–1626), *Advancement of Learning*

2 37

When you're old, and tired, and suspicious,

And plagued with doubt, you'll still hear the world calling to you.

You'll wish with all your heart you'd taken the time to listen to it.

And you'll be filled with regret.

Or maybe not.

ACG™ STANDS FOR ALL CONDITIONS GEAR BY NIKE. SHOES AND APPAREL DESIGNED FOR ANY ACTIVITY THAT TAKES PLACE OUT IN THE REAL WORLD. SHOWN HERE THE ACG DRIFTER WINDSHIRT, DESCHUTZ SHORT AND AIR MOWABB™ OUTDOOR CROSS-TRAINING SHOES. TO FIND OUT MORE, CALL 1-800-255-5ACG.

The PowerBase™ was here.

C The vastness of the white space – in contrast to the full-bleed photo – is used to describe the emptiness of life without physical activity. The contrast is further expressed by the reversed-out secondary headline in the photo.

∩ White space symbolizes a river in this logo for the fluvine city of Rotterdam.

C White space is "cleanliness" as in this three-page ad for cleaning equipment.

Representational and symbolic space

Empty space is considered extravagant, exclusive, classy. It symbolizes wealth and luxury. So leaving space empty automatically lends meaning to a design, regardless of what is being shown in the figures that lie atop it.

By injecting a disproportionate amount of space between characters and words, a self-consciously sophisticated or, conversely, an amateurish look can be given to type. A "river of white," for example, is a vertical line that becomes apparent when three or more word spaces occur above each other. This phenomenon of bad typography could be used *purposefully* to represent content in a very sophisticated way.

White space can be used to represent objects, like "river," and ideas, like "clean." Shown immediately left is the mosaic symbol for Rotterdam, illustrating the city and the Nieuwe Maas, the river which runs through it.

"Cleanliness" is symbolically shown in this opener and spread combination (facing page, bottom). The pristine white paper and unobtrusive type of the "after" view on the opening page contrasts with the cluttered "before" view, which is revealed when the page is turned.

Ideas that empty space can signify include:

Quality: extravagance, class, wealth, luxury, exclusivity

Solitude: abandonment, loneliness

Missing: lost, stolen, misplaced

Clean: bleached, washed

Purity: unsullied, unadulterated, virgin, unbuilt

Heaven: absolution, sacredness

Abundance: plenty

Openness: distance, acreage, al fresco, infinity

Calmness: placidity, undisturbed, inaction

Ice: snow, sky, day, milk, marble, river, land/water

❶ c4000BC

❷ c1800BC

❸ 842BC

❹ c150BC

3

The historical development of space:
Five timelines

c148,000BC: First human language emerges in East Africa. |
c25,000BC: Humans' earliest "writing" are paintings of objects
on cave walls. **❶** Beginning of written language. Pictographs
evolve into nonrepresentational marks. **❷** The Phoenicians develop a system that connects twenty-two spoken sounds with corresponding written symbols. **❸** First•use•of•punctuation•are

① c110

② c1450

③ c1450

④ 1460–1500

1460 Carolingian handwriting

Sibillas plurimi et max

1467 Sweynheim's "roman" typeface

Quare multarum q

1470 Jenson's "roman" typeface

E *xpectes eadem a ſ*

1500 Griffo's "italic" typeface

"How are rapid technolog-
ical advances affecting
the role of type as an
essential vehicle of com-
munication? [We redefine
a font as] a repeatable visual communication code
that can be used in an
electronic format." Baruch
Gorkin

Typefaces

Typography has been shaped by technological developments as
much as by artistic evolution. ① Stone-carvers invent serifs by finish-
ing strokes with a perpendicular hit. ② Gutenberg makes the
first movable type, styled after Textura, the dark handlettering of
his region. ③ Gutenberg's font has 290 characters including many
ligatures and contractions to justify lines. ④ Sweynheim brings
movable type to Rome, where he adopts the region's preferred
Carolingian writing style. | Jenson's "roman" type accentuates

❺ c350AD

❻ c500

❼ c800

❽ c1400

word-separating•dots. Mostwriting,though,runswordstogether. **❹** c1000BC: The Greeks and Romans adopt the Phoenician system, adding vowels and achieving even type color. **❺** After Rome's fall, writing, using parchment and vellum, is practiced in the western world almost exclusively in monasteries. **❻** One of the first codex ("book with pages") Bibles is copied near Mt Sinai. **❼** Space between words replaces•dots•between•words. Dots evolve to indicate full stops (at cap height)• and pauses (at baseline). **❽** Areas of type carved in wood are used for

"For all writing is worthwhile...according to the amount of service one gets from it." Christophe Plantin (1514–1589)

⑤ c1760

P. VIRGILII MAR

AENEID

LIBER SEXT

Sɪc fatur lacrymans: claſſiꝗue imn
Et tandem Euboicis Cumarum al
Obvertunt pelago proras: tum dente
Ancora fundabat naves, et litora curv
5 Prætexunt puppes. juvenum manus
Litus in Heſperium: quærit pars fem
Abſtruſa in venis ſilicis: pars denſa f
Tecta rapit, ſilvas; inventaꝗue flumin
At pius Aeneas arces, quibus altus A
10 Præſidet, horrendæꝗue procul ſecreta

⑥ c1815

**ABCD
KLMI
STUV
£123**

⑦ 1817

**W CAS
LETT
FOUN**

⑧ 1960s

**Abunch
character
lphabetic
order.**

ITEREST in the ... into the intre
eat Pharaoh turned horn
archaeologica lights blinke
fourth lines of Ms. Sparber,
on a mutilated could do to S
translated SCULPTURES BY RHODA SPARBER Gene Federa

**DiGiTAL
TYPEFACE
DesiGn:
More styles
& more choices**

negative space within letters for even type color. | Francesco Griffo makes the first "italic" type, basing it on cursive writing. ⑤ John Baskerville develops smooth paper, permitting his letters to be printed with greater thick-and-thin contrast. ⑥ Square serif types introduced. ⑦ First "sans serif" type available, though it takes fifteen years to be named and popularized by Vincent Figgins in London. ⑧ Phototype, developed in the 1920s, becomes widely accepted and used in the 1950s, and leads to tighter letterspacing in the 1960s because metal "shoulders" no longer exist. **END**

Computers allow anyone to design typefaces, increasing typestyle variety and interest in typography.

❾ 1455 **❿** 1478 **⓫** 1500 **⓬** 1517

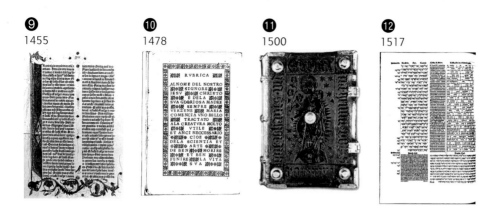

multiple rubbings. A system is needed where letters can be carved individually and duplicated so they can be quickly assembled, disassembled, and reused. **❾** Johannes Gutenberg (c1397–1468) of Mainz, Germany, advances the ability to communicate by inventing an efficient system for attaching movable letters to a printing press. Increase in printing causes reading and knowledge to become democratized. **❿** Rennaissance design using white space perfects page proportions. **⓫** In the first fifty years of printing, 35,000 books produced a total of 8–12 million copies. The

---

Punctuation's evolution includes the question mark, an abbreviated Q (from the Latin *Quaestio*), and the comma (,) in 1521; the first quote marks (" ") in France in 1557; and the first semi-colon (;) in 1569.

---

① c15,000ʙᴄ ② c1200 ③ c1450 ④ c1670

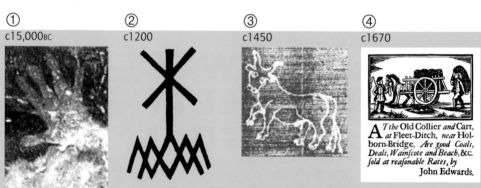

A *The* Old Collier *and* Cart, *at* Fleet-Ditch, *near* Holborn-Bridge, *Are* good Coals, Deals, *Wainscote and Beach,* &c. *sold at reasonable Rates, by* John Edwards.

Semiotics, the study of signs and meanings, defines nine categories of marks, of which these six are the most important:

1. *Representational sign,* a realistic picture of an object;

2. *Pictogram,* an iconic representation of an object;

Logos

"Logo" is Greek for "word," though it is widely used to indicate all corporate trademarks. Marks may be *symbols* (marks without type), *lettermarks* (letters form the name), *logos* (a word), or *combination marks* (symbol and logo together). ① Identifying marks have been around since the beginning of human writing, when paint was sprayed around the artist's own hand. Here, a mark from a Tasmanian cave. ② Merchant's marks are widely used to mark packages. Being diagramatic, they communicate across dialects

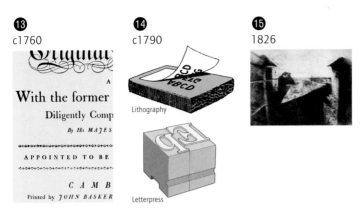

Lithography

Letterpress

average run of "incunabula" books is 250 copies. **⑫** Early grid use in G.P. de Brocar's *Polyglot Bible* accommodates five languages. **⑬** John Baskerville develops smoother paper and inks and a typeface, with pronounced thicks and thins, that takes advantage of them. **⑭** Lithography ("stone writing") is invented, based on the idea that water repels oil-based inks. Its results are more subtle than letterpress. **⑮** With photography's invention and inherent realism, printers improve continuous tones. Photoengraving is introduced in 1871. **⑯** Logically placed marginal notes liven the pages of Whistler's

> "Printing is the subject that lies at the roots of Western civilization. It's the beginning of everything, really." Stan Nelson, National Museum of American History

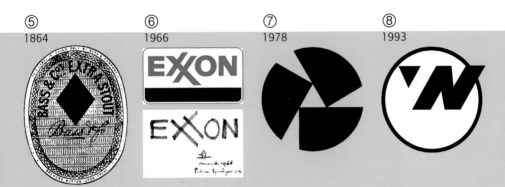

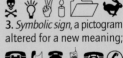

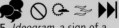

and languages. ③ The earliest watermark, a symbol embedded directly into paper fibers, is Italian from 1282. ④ With the advent of printing, "tradesman's cards" are simple, literal depictions of businesses. ⑤ Stylization is used to denote quality in the 1800s. ⑥ A logo is a mark that is a word, like *Exxon*. Shown here is Raymond Loewy's first sketch. ⑦ Abstraction is used in symbols when the companies they describe are not easily illustrated. This is for a Brazilian banking group. ⑧ A modern mark notable for its elegant *N, W,* and descriptive arrow created by negative space. **END**

3. *Symbolic sign,* a pictogram altered for a new meaning;

4. *Synonimic sign,* figures with the same referent;

5. *Ideogram,* a sign of a nonrepresentational idea;

6. *Diagram,* nonrepresentational and arbitrary.

❶⓱

¹⁸40-¹⁹00	Victorian
¹⁸50-¹⁹00	Arts & Crafts
¹⁸90-¹⁹05	Art Nouveau
¹⁹05-25	Expressionism
¹⁹10-25	Cubism
¹⁹10-45	Futurism
¹⁹15-25	Dada, De Stijl
¹⁹15-30	Constructivism
¹⁹20-35	Bauhaus
¹⁹25-40	Art Deco
¹⁹25-45	Surrealism
¹⁹30-70	Modern
¹⁹45-70	New York School
¹⁹50-	International
¹⁹60-70	Pop, Psychedelia
¹⁹70-	Basel
¹⁹75-90	Punk
¹⁹75-90	Postmodern
¹⁹90-	Global

⓲ 1918
⓳ 1919
⓴ 1923

English book. ⓱ Art movements in rapid succession throughout the twentieth century introduce visual ideas that the design community adopts. ⓲ De Stijl ("The Style") explores asymmetric type, simplicity, and dynamic divisions of space. ⓳ Cubists fragment and collage images, using letterforms as abstract elements. ⓴ Dadaists exploit shock through typographic experimentation and apparent randomness. ㉑ Constructivists combine words and pictures into a single element, often to illustrate political messages. ㉒ The Bauhaus, both the school and the philosophy, is founded

① c1842
② 1892
③ 1924
④ 1932

The earliest human markings on cave walls were posters; that is, they were messages to be seen by the artists' community. Such work today would be called murals or graffiti. That modern posters are printed on paper and hung on walls is primarily a function of printing requirements and modern mass communication.

Posters

Graphic design evolved as a profession in the mid-twentieth century from commercial artists in the trades of printing, typesetting, and illustration. ① Throughout the 1800s, printers made announcements that were, in the absence of magazines, radio, and television, a key advertising medium. ② Toulouse-Lautrec develops the poster as an art form, building on the pioneering work of fellow Parisian Jules Chéret. ③ Alexey Brodovitch launches his career with the Bal Banal poster. ④ Cassandre's posters re-

㉑ 1925

㉒ 1927

㉓ 1935

㉔ 1948

when van Doesburg partners with Gropius and Moholy-Nagy to build a new educational program in Germany. This marks the birth of graphic design as an educational discipline and as a profession. U.S. schools begin offering the subject in the late 1940s. **㉓** Herbert Matter adds extreme photographic scale to Tschichold's 1928 "New Typography" in montaged posters. **㉔** Lester Beall helps create the modern movement in New York with *Scope* magazine for Upjohn Pharmaceuticals. Beall is recognized for unifying dense scientific content with editorial simplicity and

"The art of typography, like architecture, is concerned with beauty and utility in *contemporary* terms." Bradbury Thompson (1911–1995)

⑤ 1948

⑥ 1953

⑦ 1960s

⑧ 1999

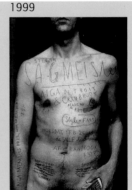

flect the cubist movement, as in this restaurant sample. **⑤** Max Huber, a Swiss living in Milan, expresses motion, speed, and noise in bright colors. **⑥** Müller-Brockmann's International style builds on the cleanliness of Swiss design. **⑦** Psychedelic posters explored malleable, distorted letterforms and organic, art nouveau expression. **⑧** Sagmeister's announcement is body-carved, accurately interpreting the mood of the U.S. street in the late 1990s. It seems to question the viability of written language itself at the turn of the millenium. **E N D**

"A poster must do two things well: to be noticed and to hold your attention long enough to get the message across. And in that order." Emil Weiss (1896–1965)

㉕
1957

Kinder verkehrs garten

㉖
1959

㉗
1975

㉘
1979

"Disputes between the traditional and modern schools of typographic thought are the fruits of misplaced emphasis. I believe the real difference lies in the way 'space' is interpreted." Paul Rand (1914-1996)

beauty. **㉕** International, or "Swiss," style grows from the Bauhaus. It uses the grid, asymmetry, and minimal typographic contrast to show hierarchy, as in Hofmann's late-50s poster. **㉖** The New York School, beginning just after World War II, is a period of extraordinary vibrancy. Art directors are given freedom to develop ways of integrating European typography with powerful, information-laden imagery. **㉗** The 1960s and 70s are decades of searching for symbolism, as shown by Glaser's I ♥ NY logo. **㉘** Self-conscious design guides the 1970s and 80s, as in this Wein-

①
1903

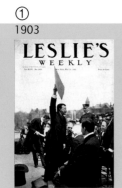

②
1929

③
1930

④
1935

Magazines

Publications evolved from leaflets to pamphlets to almanacs until 1663, when the first true magazine – offering specific information for a specific audience – was a German monthly. **①** Illustrated news weeklies that combined a balance of type and imagery proliferated with the development of industrial society. **②** Modernists transformed magazines with sans serif type and dynamic layouts, as in this early example by Joost Schmidt. **③** Henry Luce promises his new *Fortune* magazine will be "as beau-

"Whereas building is merely a matter of methods and materials, architecture implies the mastery of space." Walter Gropius (1883-1969)

㉙
1980

㉚
1992

㉛
1998

㉜
2002

gart poster. **㉙** Greiman builds on Weingart's experiments, adding video and computer references and geometric shapes as decorative elements. The computer's growing capabilities encourage exploration, often of three-dimensionality via layering. **㉚** Typographic deconstruction, the battle between legibility and maximum visual impact, as in Brody's 90s work. **㉛** Website design becomes the hot discipline through the 90s. Web-like wayfinding is applied to multipage print design. **㉜** The computer allows design from any era, but the purpose of a document remains *to be read.* **END**

"The greatness of art is not to find what is common but what is unique."
Isaac Bashevis Singer
(1904-1991)

⑤
1953

⑥
1993

tiful a magazine as exists in the U.S." **④** M.F. Agha introduces American magazine readers to the first use of sans serif type, full color photos, and full bleed images at *Vogue* and *Vanity Fair.* **⑤** Bradbury Thompson overlaps the four process colors as flat tints in his art direction of *Westvaco Inspirations.* **⑥** Fred Woodward produces a decades-long line of outstanding, expressive feature spreads for *Rolling Stone* magazine. **⑦** Magazines become a source of innovative typography as Web treatments are applied to a more sophisticated audience. **END**

⑦
2000

Section Two

Unity

designers

Reading between the lines: designers & writers

&writers

Brahms
1999

Concerto
in D
No.2

loubards du Lower East... de... Les

rêt à la fois... selon les dires d

« le blouson de cuir et le cran

fense et l'attaque en meme te

C Activated white space and dramatic cropping of letterforms make this poster's point for the AIGA NY.

C Informed use of similarity and contrast are shown in these three student projects.

U *Dwiggins coined the term *graphic designer*, wrote the first book on advertising design, and designed hundreds of books and more than eighteen typefaces.

Caledonia
Electra
Metro

4 Unity and space

Similarity and contrast 51 I Using space to create unity 55

nity contributes orderliness and coherency and a civilized state of things generally. Whereas the Contrast family are all savages, more or less. – William A. Dwiggins* (1880–1956)

One goal of graphic design is to achieve visual unity or harmony. Eugene Larkin, in the introduction to his book *Design: The Search for Unity*, writes, "The minimal requirement in visual design is... the organization of all the parts into a unified whole. All the parts, no matter how disparate, must be reconciled so they support each other." In other words, elements must be made to work together with the greatest interest *to* the reader and with the least resistance *from* the reader.

Because they had very limited resources, the earliest design practitioners achieved visual continuity rather easily: it was *externally* imposed on them by lack of choice of materials (left, top). Today, with the abundant resources available as digital information, giving designers the capability to replicate with near exactitude the work of any era, we must exercise *internal* restraint to achieve harmonious, unified design.

Similarity and contrast

Dramatic contrasts, scrupulous similarity, active white space, and a great idea are the primary attributes of well-designed documents. An environment of similarity or consistency is necessary to make a focal point visible. Planning a consistent environment is one of the most important aspects of a designer's work. Yet design consistency should not be so unchanging that it stifles creativity or becomes boring. It must express predigestion of the content to make important facets clear. Unity is achieved by joining elements and exploiting their potential relationships and alignments.

4 51

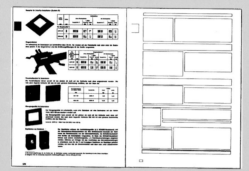

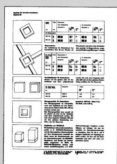

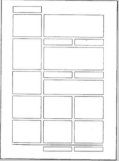

coffee with the author of Nerve Bible

Laurie Anderson

"Busy" is a word that hardly does justice to Laurie Anderson, who has been a whirlwind of activity this year: Her retrospective book Stories from Nerve Bible, was released in the spring; her new album, Bright Red, came out at the end of August; a new tour will start up by year's end. I was told I would "probably" get to interview her this Friday, provided her schedule

didn't break down. Bright Red is Anderson's most direct album since her debut, Big Science. Luckily, it didn't, and the petite woman with the deep smile lines and friendly manner greets me at the door of her office/apartment in downtown New York. Her trademark storytelling vocal style is prominent, with instrumentation and electronically altered voices kept to a minimum. And yet It turns out Anderson was as surprised by the record as anyone. "I usually write about power and authority," she laughs. After sitting across from me in a huge living room that overlooks the Hudson River, she poses the first question:

by william wansworth

C Creating contrast provides an anomaly, or focal point. The original is a cacophony of type treatments (left). By sizing and placement for similarity, the lesser elements become less visible, allowing the focal point to become clearer (right).

C ∩ Standardized column widths simplify an overly complex page. The charts above show the reduced number of column widths after the redesign.

C ∪ Image and type must share more than mere proximity. Their forms should be similar. The strongest unity is created when their meanings are fused, as in:

"The problem, not a theory nor a style, determines the solution." Karl Gerstner (1930–)

Without similarity, an environment of quietness in which important elements can be seen will not exist. On the other hand, without contrast, a design will be uneventful and uncommunicative. Achieving a balance between similarity and contrast is necessary for effective, dynamic design.

There are five ways to develop an environment of similarity:

- Keep it simple. Eliminate clutter and affect: Standardize column widths (left). Don't fill holes by inserting garbage, or at least material your reader might think is garbage. Having, say, 70 percent of your material read because you have withheld the 30 percent that is less important is far better than having only 5 percent read of *everything* you've shoved on the page.
- Build in a unique internal organization by using an unusual or eccentric grid system.
- Images and type are inherently different languages. Manipulate their shapes to create design unity. Color, texture, and direction can also be used by building on attributes of the image. More difficult – and far more effective – communication comes from unifying the meanings of images and type.
- Express continuity in a magazine from page to page and issue to issue. The handling of typographic elements, spaces between elements, rules and borders, indents, illustrations and photos, and charts and graphs should show a plan and some self-imposed limitations in formal relationships. Without such limitations, continuity can be achieved quite lazily and simply by, for example, flipping all photos upside-down. It may not be practical in everyday situations, but it is easy to see how it would unify a multipage story.
- Develop a style manual and stick with your format. Straying absorbs valuable preparation time and makes truly important variations less visible. Don't try to be different to be "creative." Worthwhile originality grows out of the special needs and materials at hand.

To make the important part stand out from its surroundings, select from the ten contrast categories shown at the top of the next page.

SPACE
filled : empty
active : passive
advancing : receding
near : far
2-D : 3-D
contained : unrestricted

POSITION
top : bottom
high : low
right : left
above : below
in front : behind
rhythmic : random
isolated : grouped
nearby : distant
centered : off center
aligned : independent
in : out

FORM
simple : complex
beautiful : ugly
abstract : representational
distinct : ambiguous
geometric : organic
rectilinear : curvilinear
symmetrical : asymmetrical
whole : broken

DIRECTION
vertical : horizontal
perpendicular : diagonal
forward : backward
stability : movement
converging : diverging
clockwise : counterclockwise
convex : concave
roman : italic

STRUCTURE
organized : chaotic
aligned : freely placed
serif : sans serif
mechanical : hand drawn

SIZE
big : little
long : short
wide : narrow
expanded : condensed
deep : shallow

COLOR
black : color
light : dark
warm : cool
bright : dull
organic : artificial
saturated : neutral

TEXTURE
fine : coarse
smooth : rough
reflective : matte
slippery : sticky
sharp : dull
fuzzy : bald

DENSITY
transparent : opaque
thick : thin
liquid : solid

GRAVITY
light : heavy
stable : unstable

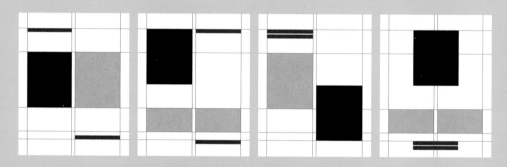

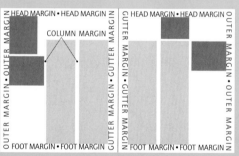

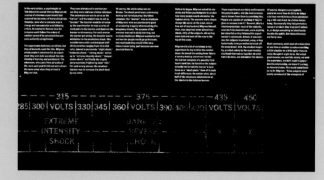

C **Every contrast pairing is an opportunity** for similarity and unity as well. For example, consistent use of bigness, instead of contrasting it with smallness, can unify a multi-spread story.

"Space is the glue, the common denominator of a visual composition." Ken Hiebert (1930–)

C **Spacing between elements should be consistent** to reduce clutter. Changing the space between the same elements produces very different results. Each of these four studies has exactly the same content.

Spaces between elements must be carefully organized or visual confusion and ambiguity result.

White space and the consistent use of type (see section 4) are the two most useful tools to create unity. Order the space between things. Elements that are physically close together look like they belong together (facing page, second row). This is the Law of Proximity. Elements that touch and overlap look even more related. To create design unity, spaces between elements should be equal and consistent in a design.

Use white space on the perimeters of designs – in outside margins, head sinkage, and column bottoms – where it is visible and where it will aid in defining the design's personality.

Margins are the spaces around the perimeter of a page (facing page, third row). They are the frame around the "live area." Wide outer margins may be used for attention-getting graphics like small images and secondary display type. A gutter is the space between columns of type and between pages in a bound document. Space between columns should not be so narrow as to be mistaken for a word space, yet not so wide that they become an interruption. Text should generally have a one-pica column space. Rag right text may have a smaller column space.

Head sinkage is the consistent deep space at the top of a page or design (facing page, third row). It can be increased on selected pages in a publication to make them stand apart, or it can be used consistently as a place in which to put display type and small images.

Column bottoms may be left uneven (facing page, bottom) if their unevenness looks purposeful. Uneven column bottoms, also called scalloped columns, must differ in length by at least three lines. Uneven white space at the bottoms of columns is unobstrusive and makes editing easier.

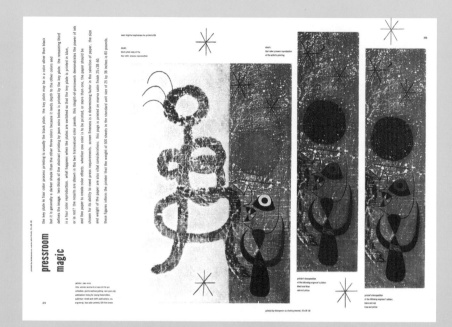

pressroom
magic

the key plate in four color process printing is usually the black plate. the key plate may be in a color other than black but it is generally a darker shade than the other three colors because it needs depth to the other colors and defines this image. two-thirds of the abstract printing by pann miro below is printed by the key plate. the remaining third in a four color reproduction. what happens when the plates are switched so that the key plate is printed in blue, or in red? the results are shown in the two translucent color panels. this sleight-of-presswork demonstrates the power of ink and fine paper to create color effects. whether one color is to be printed, or more than one, the paper should be chosen for its ability to meet press requirements. screen fineness is a determining factor in the selection of paper. the size and weight of the paper are also vital considerations. this page is printed on manse satin finish 25x38-60. these figures inform the printer that the weight of 500 sheets in the standard unit size of 25 by 38 inches is 60 pounds.

painter: joan miro
title: woman and bird in band of the sun
collection: pierre matisse gallery, new york city
publication: living for young homemakers
publisher: street and smith publications, inc.
engraving: four color process, 120 line screen

new virginia loghshakes inc priletto 06

detail:
black plate only of his
four color process reproduction

detail:
four color process reproduction
of the artist's painting

printer's transposition
of the following engraver's plates:
black and blue
red and yellow

printed by letterpress on sterling enamel, 25x38-60

printer's transposition
of the following engraver's plates:
black and red
blue and yellow

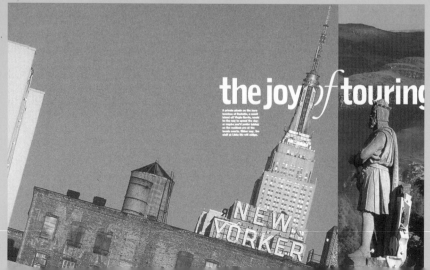

the joy of touring

A private plane on the barn lawnlow of Oakville, a small island off Virgin Gorda, could be the way to spend the day; or maybe you'd prefer taking on the comfort pro of the bands courts. Either way, the staff at Little Dix will oblige.

NEW
YORKER

5 The seven design components

*T*he essence of taste is suitability. Divest the word of its prim and priggish implications, and see how it expresses the mysterious demand of the eye and mind for symmetry, harmony, and order. – Edith Wharton (1862-1937)

⌒ **The huge size** of the UNITY above represents its position of supreme importance in design.

⊂ Visual unity is shown in a series of design elements that share verticality (top). Conceptual unity is expressed in a group of objects found, for example, at the beach (middle). A designer must often unify elements that do not share visual characteristics (bottom).

"The whole point of composing is to make the result seem inevitable." Aaron Copland (1900– 1990)

"The most difficult things to design are the simplest." Raymond Loewy (1893-1986)

Wolfgang Weingart, the Swiss designer and design educator, said, "I am convinced that...investigation of elementary typographic exercises is a prerequisite for the solution of complex typographic problems." That point is equally valid with reference to *design* problems.

This chapter describes the elementary design components. Mastering them will produce exceptional results regardless of the design problem's complexity.

Unity

Unity in design exists when all elements are in agreement. Elements are made to look like they belong together, not as though they happened to be placed randomly. Unity requires that the whole design be more important than any subgroup or individual part. Unity is therefore the goal of all design. It is the most important aspect of design, so important that its achievement excuses any design transgression.

Unity exists in elements that have a visual similarity – in, for example, elements that are all vertical (left, top). Unity also exists in elements that have a conceptual similarity, as shown in the collection of things that can be found at the beach (left, center).

Similitude can be carried too far, resulting in a unified but dull design. Contrastingly, little similarity between elements will dazzle, but the design – and the message it is trying to communicate – will not be unified. So, without *unity* a design becomes chaotic and unreadable. But without *variety*, a design becomes

❶

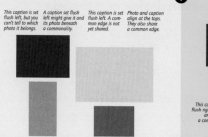
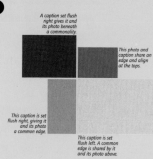

❷

❸

❹

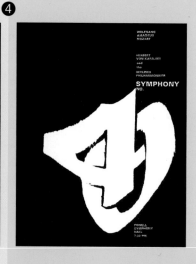

⊂ There are four ways of relating elements to achieve unity (examples in the right column show more effective treatments):

❶ **Proximity:** Elements that are physically close are seen as related. At far left, the elements are seen as two groups, captions and images. On the right, each caption is correctly joined to its image.

❷ **Similarity:** Elements that share similar position, size, color, shape, or texture are seen as related and grouped.

❸ **Repetition:** Recurring position, size, color, and use of graphic elements create unity.

❹ **Theme with variations:** Alteration of a basic theme retains connectedness while providing interest. In this example the theme is small type set flush left.

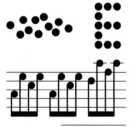

⌒ **Random dots** (top left) can be arranged to convey a message, making their sum different from *and more important than* their individual features.

inert, lifeless, and uninteresting. A balance must be found between the two.

All formal relationships – relationships between forms, not relationships in evening dress – must be created so that unity among the parts is achieved. This can be accomplished by manipulating proximity, similarity, repetition, and theme with variations:

Proximity (also called *grouping* or *relative nearness*): The simplest way to achieve unity. Elements that are physically close together are seen as related. The further apart they are separated, the less they appear to be related.

Similarity (also called *correspondence*): Elements that share similarity of size, color, shape, position, or texture are seen as alike. The reverse of similarity is intentional contrast: type or imagery that is bigger is seen as more important. Alignment is an especially significant aspect of similarity in which elements that line up with one another appear related.

Repetition (related to *similarity*): Any idea that is repeated provides unity. The repeated idea may be positioning, size, color, or use of rules, background tints, and boxes. Repetition produces rhythm.

Theme with variations: Simple repetition without variety can become boring in its sameness. Alteration of a basic theme retains connectedness while providing interest.

Gestalt

Gestalt is a German term, coined at the Staatliches Bauhaus in Weimar in the early 1920s, that describes a design's wholeness: *A design's unity is more than the simple addition of its parts.* In other words, each part of a design is affected by what surrounds it. By manipulating the interaction of the individual parts, you affect the *cumulative perception* (page 60). Gestalt is the overall quality being described when you say, "This design *works*."

When we look at a building or a painting or a magazine spread, we perceive it first as a whole because the eye automatically seeks wholeness and unity. Rudolf Arnheim, psychologist and

❶

❷

❸

žijeme 1931

ANHALTISCHER
KUNSTVEREIN
JOHANNISSTR. 13

GEMÄLDE AQUARELLE

KANDINSKY

JUBILÄUMS-AUSSTELLUNG

60.
GEBURTSTAG

Geöffnet:	Wochentags: 2 - 5 nachm.
	Mittwoch u. Sonntag 11 - 1
Eintritt:	Mitglieder: Frei
	Nichtmitglieder: 50 Pfg.

⟲ Gestalt describes individual elements relating as a unified whole in these three ways (examples on right show more effective treatments):

❶ Figure/ground: Ambiguity between a subject and its surrounding space.

❷ Completion or closure: Unfinished forms can be seen as whole (right). They intrigue and involve the viewer more than stable, complete shapes.

❸ Continuation: The eye follows a path, whether it is real or implied, as shown with the separated head.

Now that's flying first class.

◠ Closure is illustrated in the apparent randomness of the flying birds. On closer inspection, our eyes "connect the dots" and we see that the birds are arranged in the shape of the sponsor's trademark.

⟲ Gestalt principles are expressed in these Bauhaus designs. Far left: Ladislav Sutnar's cover for a magazine. Left: Herbert Bayer's 1926 poster for a colleague's sixtieth birthday.

art theoretician, writes in *Visual Thinking*, "We see the various components, the shapes and colors and the relations between them.... The observer receives the total image as the result of the interaction among the components. This interaction...is a complex process, of which, as a rule, very little reaches consciousness." But, he says, there is an alternative way of seeing. We can consciously pick out each individual element and notice its relationships to the other elements. Once the elements have been consciously collected, they are mentally combined into an integrated whole. The first process is intuitive. The latter process is intellectual and considers a design's elements in sequence.

For example, if you listen to recorded versions of the same movement of a piece of orchestral music, you will hear nuances and subtle differences between them, even though the same notes are being played. Their *totality*, their *wholeness* differs, and that is musical gestalt.

Either process results in a complete perception by the viewer. The techniques for manipulating that perception include the four unity ideas described on the previous page, as well as the following three ideas.

Figure/ground: The relationship of the subject to its surrounding space. Confusing the foreground and background is a visually stimulating technique.

Closure (also called *completion*): The viewer's natural tendency is to try to close gaps and complete unfinished forms. Closure encourages active participation in the creation of the message.

Continuation: The arrangement of forms so they are "continuous" from one element to another, leading the eye across space. Continuation also can lead from one page to another.

Gestalt, or cumulative perception, helps us see a significant message in the arrangement of the dots in the illustration on the preceding page. In a more complex way, gestalt helps us understand the message revealed in a group of images and words designed as a magazine story.

C Dominance: Manipulating sizes so one element overwhelms another affects meaning, as shown by this four-step process. Unexpected dominance can make an ordinary idea seem fresh.

C Scale: Readers perceive an element as being "small" or "big" in comparison to nearby elements and to natural human size.

∩ Hierarchy is best expressed through proximity, grouping less important things near each other and putting one thing apart **and C similarity,** making all things alike. If all elements are too similar, even in their specialness – as shown in this Wiley Miller *Non Sequitur* cartoon – the only way to make a focal point is by making it plain.

Space

Consider white space in relation to the other design components of unity, gestalt, dominance, hierarchy, balance, and color as *primus inter pares* ("first among equals").

To avoid a stale approach to organizing elements on the page, look at the blank area you start with and think of displacing the emptiness with pictures, display and text type, and graphic embellishments like rules. Stay conscious of the remaining empty areas and use it to guide, attract, and arouse the viewer to become engaged.

Dominance

Dominance is closely related to contrast, since there must be contrast for one element to dominate another. Dominance is created by contrasting size (also called *scale*), positioning, color, style, or shape.

Lack of dominance among a group of equally-weighted elements forces competition among them. Readers must then discover their own entry point, which is a chore. Generally speaking, every design should have a single primary visual element, known as a focal point, which dominates the designscape. Readers then have an obvious starting point and are more easily guided to subsequent levels of a information.

Scale, or relative size, is described by English sculptor Henry Moore: "We relate everything to our own [human] size." Scale can be used to attract attention by making the focal point life size or, for even more drama, larger-than-life size. Consciously reversing the sizes of adjacent elements is also arresting.

Hierarchy

The best design moves the reader across the page in order of the type and images' significance. Content is best expressed as most important, least important, and all the remaining information made equivalently important. Having more than three levels of information is confusing because, while it may be clear what is *most* important and what is *least* important, it is rarely clear what the significant difference is between middling material.

5 **63**

"But he cuts off his nose to spite his face!"

"Why does he do it, Doctor? That man is obsessed with his corporate image and yet he continually presents less than his best face to the public.

"He spends millions of dollars for advertising space and as little as he can for what fills that space. We come up with great ideas. He buys them. We present estimates. He slashes them. Between the great ideas and the great ads a great deal gets lost in the translation.

"He's actually more concerned with the charge for photostats than the charge people will get from his advertising. In television, the syndrome is the same with the symptoms on a much larger scale. And in point-of-sale and direct mail, his company appearance is even more embarrassing.

"Sure, I realize that he has a strong urge for self-destruction. I know it's *his* problem but what can be done to help him?"

Psychiatry might help. But it's probably too late. You will have to get him to face the facts of life. That there's nothing as expensive as advertising that just misses. SH&L has helped convince men like this to take a new look at their advertising. Call Dr. Lubalin at PL 1-1250 or leave a message with his nurse.

⌒ Asymmetrical balance Using page perimeter and bleed to emphasize the left edge of a spread forces the reader to look back and forth from the missing nose to the headline. They are equivalent in attention-getting weight in this ad designed by Herb Lubalin. Note that the nose and headline are horizontally aligned, strengthening their relatedness.

⌒ Symmetrical balance looks classical, though static, on this carefully crafted cover by Canadian designer Tony Sutton.

⌒ "Overall balance," used to great effect in Katie Schofield's digital painting *Transparent Alphabet #4*, is similar to wallpaper. It lacks both a focal point and hierarchy. Overall balance is often used by retailers who want to pack maximum information into their advertising space.

"When in doubt, make it red. If you're still in doubt, make it big." Ivan Chermayeff (1932–)

Our eyes respond to elements' relative nearness and similarities, so repeat the same shape (or color or type) to guide the reader to corresponding elements.

Balance

Balance, or equilibrium, is the state of equalized tension. It is not necessarily a state of calm. There are three types of balance. Symmetrical, or formal, balance is vertically centered and is visually equivalent on both sides. Symmetrical designs are static and evoke feelings of classicism, formality, and constancy.

Asymmetrical, or informal, balance attracts attention and is dynamic. Asymmetry requires a variety of element sizes and careful distribution of white space. Because they have more complex relationships, it takes sensitivity and skill to handle elements asymmetrically. Asymmetrical designs evoke feelings of modernism, forcefulness, and vitality.

The third type of balance is overall, or mosaic, balance. This is usually the result of too much being forced on a page. Overall balance lacks hierarchy and meaningful contrast. It is easy for this type of organization to look "noisy." For that reason, some elements should be placed elsewhere or deleted.

Balance is an important route to achieving unity in design. If the various elements are seen to be in balance, the design will look unified. It will make a single impression. If a design is out of balance, its constituent parts will be more visible than the overall design.

Color

Color is partly artistry but mostly science and common sense. Like good writing and good design, good color is a raw material to be used strategically for a clear purpose. Color contrast has the same potential for communicating hierarchy as typeface, type weight and size, or placement contrasts. Random application or changes in color work against the reader's understanding just as do any random changes in design.

As a functional way to help guide the reader, color:

■ **Aids organization**, establishing character through consistency. Develop a color strategy. Limit color use as you limit

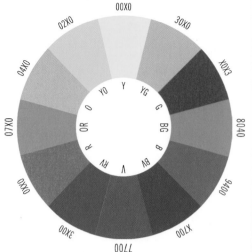

Hues are colors, like red, yellow, and green.

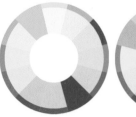

■ **Complementary colors** are opposite each other.

■ **Analogous colors** are next to each other on the color wheel.

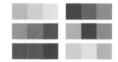

■ **Shades** are made by adding black, which reduces saturation.

■ **Tints** are made by adding white, which reduces saturation.

■ **Value** is the lightness or darkness of a color.

■ **Saturation** *or* chroma *or* intensity is the brightness or dullness of a color.

■ **Triadic harmonies** are three colors that are equidistant.

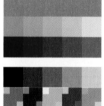

■ **Monochromatic color** is a single hue with tints and shades. **Achromatic colors** are black, white, and grays, which can be made by mixing complementary colors.

WORDS
SYMBOLS
CONSCIOUSNESS
COLOR

🎧 **Marshall McLuhan's three-level "hierarchy of communication."** Color is at the bottom, functioning in the viewer's subconscious. Above it are symbols and signs, and at the top are words.

Colors have particular associations, according to Dr. Max Luescher, a Swiss psychologist. These general associations must be tempered by context and application.

BLUE	DIGNIFIED
GREEN	PERSISTENT
RED	ASSERTIVE
YELLOW	OPTIMISTIC
BROWN	PASSIVE
VIOLET	MEDITATIVE
BLACK	SURRENDER
GRAY	BARRIER

A practical guide is to use color's relative temperature to make elements come forward or recede. All colors are relatively warmer or cooler, depending on what they are next to. **Red and yellow** pop forward. **Blue** and **green** recede.

C **Use less color (left) rather than more (right)** or your readers will have a colorful mess to decipher. Color should be used in the same way that type size is used: to emphasize importance, not decorate the page.

font use to communicate real differences. ☐ Plan color use from the start. If it is added on at the end, its use is most likely to be only cosmetic. ☐ Use color consistently. Along with typography and spacing attributes, a unique color scheme can be an identifying characteristic.

■ **Gives emphasis**, ranking elements in order of importance. Regardless of ink color used, every element has a color – or perceptual emphasis – that must be considered. Type itself is said to have "color," or gray value, that can be used to create hierarchy. Darker type is seen first, so display type is usually bolder and bigger. ☐ Color highlights elements of importance. You read this first, didn't you? ☐ Color codes information, simplifying complex data. ☐ Color's highlighting benefit is quickly exhausted and devolves into a colorful mess. ☐ People gravitate to whatever looks different on a page.

■ **Provides direction**, relating parts to each other. Warm colors move elements forward while cool colors move elements back, so a warm tone should be given to display type that is in front of an image to further the illusion of spatiality. ☐ Use graduated tints since there are no flat colors in nature.

Printed color is affected by "ink holdout," the ability of paper to keep ink on the surface and not dissipate by soaking in. Coated papers have high ink holdout and make photos look much sharper. The extra processing makes coated papers cost more. Paper with the lowest ink holdout is the paper towel, whose very purpose is to absorb.

Black type on white paper has the most contrast possible. Any color applied to type will make the type weaker. Counteract this effect by increasing type weight from book to regular or from regular to semibold, and increase type size for optical equivalency.

Everyone perceives light and color a little differently and with their own set of subconscious associations. But all readers respond to usefulness of information. Analyze, define what's useful to the reader, and point out its potential value with color and the six other design components.

Raum braucht der Mensch

Der Mensch sehnt sich nach Weite und
Freiheit. Doch meist ist er eingekeilt: auf der
Straße, in den Ferien, bei der Arbeit, in
seiner Wohnsituation. Deshalb ist es heute
wichtiger denn je, sich auch privaten
Freiraum zu schaffen. Ob im Haus mit
Garten oder einer geräumigen Eigentums-
wohnung: Als Hypothekenbank können
wir Ihnen dabei helfen, sich den Raum
zu schaffen, den Sie sich wünschen.
München. Telefon: 089/5112-371/287.

SÜDDEUTSCHE BODENCREDITBANK
AKTIENGESELLSCHAFT   HYPOTHEKENBANK

München Berlin Dortmund Dresden Düsseldorf Erfurt Frankfurt/Main Freiburg Hamburg Hannover Leipzig Stuttgart

Space is what man needs

Man longs for distance and freedom. But mostly he is wedged in:
on the street, on vacation, at work,
in his living environment. That is
why it is more important than ever
today to get some personal space.
Whether it is the house or the garden
or a spacious condo apartment: as a
mortgage bank we can help you create the space you wish for. Munich.

South German Bodencreditbank

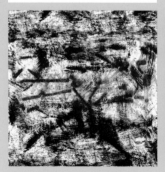

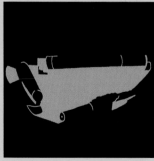

C All parts must fit together. This German bank ad uses space, abstraction, dominance, hierarchy, and color to excellent effect, that is, to illustrate the very concept of the ad.

◯ Join elements to make a unified design. At left is a naive drawing of eyes, ears, and mouth on a head. On the right, the head in its entirety is more important than its individual elements.

C Simplify by thinking of design elements as shapes. Designers learn how to see abstractly by replacing naturalistic elements with points, lines, and planes.

"...A building is not designed by putting together a series of rooms. Any (good) building has an underlying design concept that binds all the parts together into a whole. Without this it is not architecture." Edmund N. Bacon (1910-)

6 How to use the seven design components

Think of shapes 71 **I** Design evolves 73

I define beauty to be a harmony of all the parts...
fitted together with such proportion and
connection, that nothing could be added,
diminished or altered, but for the worse.
– Leon Battista Alberti (1406–1472)

The seven design components – unity, gestalt, space, dominance, hierarchy, balance, and color – are sliding switches, like a lamp's dimmer, that help achieve visible, effective design (left). While you may choose to have more or less of each of these components, it isn't possible to select just one and not use the others. They come bundled as a group.

Good design necessitates that one element dominate the others in the context of a cumulative perception, or gestalt. Choosing that emphasis suggests a design's starting point. Balance one large or bright element against a few smaller or muted ones.

Function in design is paramount. What is the message? Choose pictures that tell the story. Use color to show what is important. Motivate the reader by arranging the elements in a logical hierarchy. The top left corner of every page or spread is a valuable starting point because readers look there first. Exploit the reader's natural habits.

The purpose of design is emphatically not to fill up all the space. Don't let overabundance make the information in your design impenetrable. As Steven Ledbetter, music historian and critic, wrote, "Beethoven's control of relative tension and relative relaxation throughout the gigantic architectural span [of the first movement of his Symphony No.3] remains one of the most awe-inspiring accomplishments in the history of music."

Organize elements so all parts fit together to make a unified whole. Find design unity in the elements' commonalities. Organize elements by their shared subject matter, shape, or color.

O mam e a casa do teatro apresentam

Espetáculo inspirado na
obra de Clarice Lispector

Quase
de Verdade

Direção: Ulisses Cohn • Elenco: Cia Delas

Domingos às 11:00h
mam
auditório Lina Bo Bardi
Parque do Ibirapuera

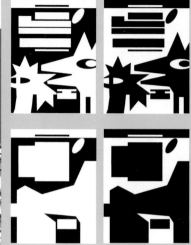

♪ Create a buffer zone that uses surrounding white space. Interrupt a thick white border on each side to make your space look bigger than it actually is. This technique is used by artist Summer Jellison in her "Glass Owl."

C Top row: Students learn to see letters as shape. Each of these studies uses a single letter.
Bottom row: A letterform and textures are combined on a grid. Attention to white space is emphasized.

"At the definition stage of a project, we are less concerned with what it will look like and more concerned with what it will be." John Ormsbee Simonds, *Landscape Architecture*

Designers have different sensibilities and preferences, which is why five designers given the same pictures and copy would create five different designs. But given a single message to get across, we expect they would develop comparable solutions.

Think of shapes

Readers operate subconsciously on these design truisms:

■ We read from left to right.

■ We start at the top and work down the page.

■ Pages in a publication are related to each other.

■ Closeness connects while distance separates.

■ Big and dark is important; small and light is less important.

■ Fullness should be balanced with emptiness.

■ Everything has a shape, including emptiness.

Design is, among other things, the arrangement of shapes. Experiment by mentally setting aside the meaning of headlines, copy, visuals, and other elements and treat them as if they were purely shapes (facing page, top). Henry Moore, the English sculptor, said, "The sensitive observer of [design] must feel shape simply as shape, not as a description or idea. He must, for example, perceive an egg as a simple solid shape, quite apart from its significance as food, or from the idea that it will become a bird."

Shapes exist in the realm of figure and ground only. Try overlapping and clustering shapes to create visually interesting concentrations. To simplify a design, reduce the total number of shapes by joining two or three at a time.

Letterforms are shapes that can be exploited in display typography and logo design. It is necessary to see the form of letters before complex typographic ideas can be developed (facing page, bottom). Without exploiting letters' individual forms and the shape of the space around and within letterforms, the only option is mere typesetting in groups of letters and words.

White space, within type and around columns and pictures, must be considered as a shape. Push it in chunks to the perimeter or to the bottom of the page.

1

When Forgiving Is Hard

Monday, November 25, 2004

Read Psalm 19:7—14

Forgive us our debts, as we forgive our debtors.
— Matthew 6:12 (KJV)

EACH time we say the Lord's prayer, we repeat that request to forgive; but how often are we called upon to really act on that simple plea?

My mother was recently attacked in her home in the middle of the night. Though she was not seriously injured, she was roughed up and robbed. When I heard about what had happened, my immediate reaction was one of rage as I thought of her fear and humiliation. Several days later, however, the thought came to me that as Christians we are charged to forgive those who act against us.

Sometimes praying for our enemies is hard, almost impossible; but the Lord did so and wants us to do the same. Each day, I concentrate on offering up these unknown assailants, praying also that the feelings in my heart will match the words on my lips.

PRAYER: Forgiving God, please grant that the meditations of our heart and the words on our lips will be acceptable in Your sight. In Christ□s name. Amen.

THOUGHT FOR THE DAY

If we do not feel forgiving, we can pray that our feelings will change.

Tuck Eudy (Georgia)

28   PRAYER FOCUS: Those who have wronged us

2

When Forgiving Is Hard

28   **Monday, November 25, 2004**

Read Psalm 19:7—14

Forgive us our debts, as we forgive our debtors.
— Matthew 6:12 (KJV)

EACH time we say the Lord's prayer, we repeat that request to forgive; but how often are we called upon to really act on that simple plea?

My mother was recently attacked in her home in the middle of the night. Though she was not seriously injured, she was roughed up and robbed. When I heard about what had happened, my immediate reaction was one of rage as I thought of her fear and humiliation. Several days later, however, the thought came to me that as Christians we are charged to forgive those who act against us.

Sometimes praying for our enemies is hard, almost impossible; but the Lord did so and wants us to do the same. Each day, I concentrate on offering up these unknown assailants, praying also that the feelings in my heart will match the words on my lips.

PRAYER: Forgiving God, please grant that the meditations of our heart and the words on our lips will be acceptable in Your sight. In Christ□s name. Amen.

THOUGHT FOR THE DAY

If we do not feel forgiving, we can pray that our feelings will change.

Tuck Eudy (Georgia)

PRAYER FOCUS: Those who have wronged us

3

When forgiving is hard

28   Monday, November 25, 2004

Read Psalm 19:7–14

Forgive us our debts, as we forgive our debtors.
– Matthew 6:12 (KJV)

EACH time we say the Lord's prayer, we repeat that request to forgive; but how often are we called upon to really act on that simple plea?

My mother was recently attacked in her home in the middle of the night. Though she was not seriously injured, she was roughed up and robbed. When I heard about what had happened, my immediate reaction was one of rage as I thought of her fear and humiliation. Several days later, however, the thought came to me that as Christians we are charged to forgive those who act against us.

Sometimes praying for our enemies is hard, almost impossible; but the Lord did so and wants us to do the same. Each day, I concentrate on offering up these unknown assailants, praying also that the feelings in my heart will match the words on my lips.

Prayer Forgiving God, please grant that the meditations of our heart and the words on our lips will be acceptable in Your sight. In Christ's name. Amen.

Thought for the day If we do not feel forgiving, we can pray that our feelings will change.

Tuck Eudy *Georgia*

Prayer focus Those who have wronged us

Design evolves

Uncovering and recognizing design relationships takes time. Just as when we walk into a dark room, it takes time to accustom our eyes to the materials at hand.

Design must evolve from basic relationships to more complex, more refined relationships. Start the process by becoming intimately familiar with the content. Read every word of the text. Understand *what* is being said. Understand, too, *why* it was written and why it is being published. Then find out *who* is going to read it and what the reader's motivation is. Finally, develop a strategy for expressing it to the reader's greatest advantage.

Design evolution should proceed on two levels simultaneously. One is to seek relationships of *meaning*, which appeals to the reader's need for understanding. The other is to seek relationships of *form*, which appeals to the reader's need for attraction. Balancing these two ensures effective visual communication.

Design is spoiled more often by the designer's having been overly cautious rather than having been overly bold. Dare to be bold.

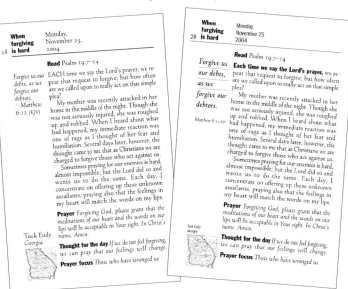

Section
Three

Page Architecture

KOLIN

中國的月亮不很圓……

ZEITSCHRIFT FÜR KULTUR
WIRTSCHAFT UND LITERATUR

PREIS 1 MARK

USSR

DAS NEUE RUSSLAND

DOPPELHEFT 8/9
BERLIN
NOVEMBER 1931

Kepes

⌒ *Purple Robe and Anemones*, painted in 1937, shows Matisse's comprehensive use of space.

☾ **Architecture and design share visual structure.** At top left, symmetry is shown in Eliel and Eero Saarinen's 1941 Berkshire Opera Shed and, beneath it, a Chinese newspaper ad. At top right, asymmetry in Jaipur's Samrat Yantra, an eighteenth-century astronomical structure, and, near left, in a 1931 cover by Gyorgy Kepes.

☾ **Architecture and calligraphy use** active positive and negative space, as in this 1575 Turkish calligraphy (far left) and ☽ a Mexican resort hotel.

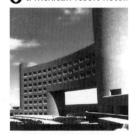

7
The page as visual structure

Architecture and design 87 I Chains of thought 93 I Grids: Freedom in structure 93

T he whole arrangement of my picture is expressive. The place occupied by the figures or objects, the empty spaces around them, the proportions, everything plays a part. – Henri Matisse (1869-1954), *Notes d'un peintre*

A chicken's skeleton. Stud and beam construction. The design grid. Each of these is an unseen substructure on which visible, external parts are draped and attached. The chicken's skeleton is covered, for example, by muscles, skin, and feathers. The modern house has wallboard, flooring, and shingles. A design has words and pictures. In each case, the substructure determines the placement of the visible elements.

Architecture and design

A completely new way of realizing large-scale architecture occurred in the mid-thirteenth century. Construction of the church of St.-Denis, near Paris, had stopped about eighty years earlier when the abbot who began the building died. When the church's new design was proposed in 1231, it was the first instance of Rayonnant ("radiant") architecture, in which radiating patterns of cut-glass windows flooded the building with light. It was a purposeful decision to have empty space *within* the cathedral be more important than the stone walls that surrounded the space.

Harry Sternberg wrote, "In architecture the structural beams support the walls, floors, piping, and wiring, as well as the facade of the building. In any graphic work...composition is the basic structure which supports all the other elements involved."

There has always been a similiarity between architecture and design in thinking style and problem–solving approach. Hassan Massoudy said in his 1986 book *Calligraphy*, "An architectural

Everything has an end.

Except a wurst. O, for draught of vintage! That hath been cool'd a long age in the deep-delved earth, tasting of flora and the country green, dance and Provencal song, and so sunburnt mirth! O for the warm, warm South. **That has two.**

G U S T A V   M A H L E R

Everything has an end, except a wurst.

O, for draught of vintage! That hath been cool'd a long age in the deep-delved earth, tasting of flora and the country mirth! O for a beaker full of the warm, blushful South. O, for draught of vintage! That hath been cool'd a long age in the deep-dance and Provencal song, and so sunburnt beak full of the warm, country green to taste of flora and the country green, dance and sing the Provencal song, and so sunburnt mirth for a bucket full of the warm, blushful draught of vintage that hath been cool'd a long age in the deep-delved earth, tasting of flora and the country green, so sunburnt mirth! O for a beaker full of the warm, warm South.

That has two.

Everything *has* an end except a wurst

That has *two* *two*

O, for draught of vintage! That hath been cool'd a long age in the deep-delved earth, tasting of flora and the country green, dance and Provencal song, and so sunburnt mirth! O for a beaker full of the warm, blushful south. **GUSTAV MAHLER**

C "Architectural space can be fluid or static; additive or divisive; positive or negative; colorful or monochromatic." - Kohei Ishikawa. Solid space, or volume, shown in three buildings (top row), and architectural emptiness, or voids (second row).

* Cesar Pelli, architect of City Centre, says, "The space between the buildings is the most important part of this design. These are the only skyscrapers that emphasize negative space. It is a portal to the sky, to the clouds, to God."

C Castles illustrate layout complexity:

SIMPLE

Primitive	=	Elementary
castle		page
		architecture

STANDARD

Regular	=	Intermediate
castle		page
		architecture

COMPLEX

Elaborate	=	Intricate
castle		page
		architecture

"Architecture is the beautiful and serious game of space." Willem Dudok (1884–1974)

design defines a living space; the space between the walls is as real and as significant as the walls themselves. In [graphic design] the value of a space derives from its relationship with the [elements] that surround it and vice versa." Sean Morrison, in *A Guide to Type Design*, says, "Type designers are closer to architects than to artists. The architect must produce a building that is structurally sound and efficient but that is also visually pleasing and comfortable to live and work in." Surely, a designer's work must conform to these same requirements to be useful.

Architectural volumes are created as either solid (space displaced by mass), or void (space contained or enclosed by planes). Solid volumes are buildings: St. Mawes Castle, England; Il Duomo, Firenze; and Seafair, a Newport, Rhode Island, mansion. Voids are spaces defined by solids: The space between the towers of the world's tallest buildings, the Kuala Lumpur City Centre, Malaysia*; the interior of Il Duomo, Siena; and the Piazza Cisterna, San Gimignano, Italy.

A building's purpose and size are the architect's first considerations. Similarly, determining a document's purpose and its page size are the first decisions a designer must make. The page's size and its shape create reader expectations: a square or horizontal page immediately signals an unusual document. A standard 8½" x 11" vertical page (or European A4) must overcome its size and shape to be recognized as remarkable. The designer must also weigh technical issues: economies of printing (a really great two-color job is far better than an inferior four-color job) and paper buying (trimming excess paper to get an unusual shape costs money), binding, standard envelope sizes, size requirements imposed by the post office, postage, even what size fits best on the computer screen at full-size and full-screen view.

According to architect Kohei Ishikawa, "The placement of windows and doors defines the function of rooms." The page size and the layout signal the type of document the reader is holding. What makes a bound document a book versus a magazine? What distinguishes a newsletter from a newspaper? What makes

Left newsletter

Volume 6, Number 3

Environmental
NEWS

The Monthly Newsletter
of The Mid-State Ecology Group

Members E-Mail

If Grupo members go members have using the fax by the fax donate president, Clyde Hank such regularity regularity that have to purchase purchase an additional torational toreal of ti paper. That as, r. That is, as Pre Clyde Hanks saw Hanks says, "u of our generouer generous memb wons rantribes contribues t for our cause "ar cause."

Treasurer Oustourer Guy Douln several gif'as meral gif'as made ti over the past t the past, few ger complete endabless enabling kit filler table writh table with brag waders in a julers t

T-shirts a Hit

More If Grupo t-po t-shirts how sold in the past past march that our entire histohistory, repor ta President. Sergiemp Horal. Cal from the kitchkitchen of his re rant, Segei's, or S, or fast 56th Street, Serge Serge tells us that shirts have beee been selling su week at the erak erak tonsters storks in lower lower Manhattan.

Across the cove country, Serg his stoff of gear tea oceoe stor tweel large star sizes and bright colors. All proceorceeds from t sales benefit this

2003
34/sq acre

Down 24% in two years

2005
26/sq acre

Crab Count Down

For the senthe second year in a the crab cemub count in Foster ts substantistantially lower th previous geous year. Friends o Bay taffed taffled their annual in the thirthe third week of Feb and found tfound the stock of f szent erabat erabs had dropped sinte fast ye fast year, and 23% the year begear before shut.

"This is lers is terrible news," Clyde Hankse Hanks, chapter pri "How can th can the spawning u make up the up the ground ther over the fit the last two years' will have tonave to stop on twel harvesting vesting until furthe tine." Mayor Mayor Afbrenht is

the end of tend of the month. U then, ne vn, we urge all If Grupo bers to dise to discontineu cral catching wheng until we can ac our phrone cfrone tree sys:

chard Wuard Walton, directo the Corsne Corsanenal School Aquacultuulturoe in North H soid, "I have "I have nat get read report, burt, but the early we that is fork ts fork s meghig grt craba steeuo steamed, stuffed it doesn't meon't matter from m get our endur crabs in future, thus they s they ore fresh und clean, fresh, fresh, brackish w ts appears tspears thus I'll have fresh frosh froten from the Y like the reshe rest

An emergenmergency meeting Crab Subta Subcommettee ts pl for the tmehe tmelft

---

Right newsletter

The Monthly Newsletter of The Mid-State Ecology Group

Environmental
NEWS

Volume 6, Number 3

2003
34/sq acre

Down 24% in two years

2005
26/sq acre

Members e-mail

If Grupo membe members have beer using the to the fax donated by president, Client, Clyde Hanks, wit such regularegularity that we n have to purto purchase several additional totoral boral of theme. paper. That, That is, as Presiden Clyde Hanks Hanks says, "unless o of our genergenerous members s up wns orntan contribuies the pa for our cause cause."

Treasurer tsurer Guy Douflin oug several gif'as gif'as made to if Gri over the phethe past two years c complete cruse crabbing kits a cr filler table viable with bray and waders in a sin a full range

T-shirts a hit

More If Grupo If Grupo t-shirts to how sold in the pn the past month tha our entire histne histre history, report the President Sdent Sergie Horal. Cal from the kitke kitchhen of his re rant, Segei's Segei's or fast 56th Street, Gergii, Gergii, Serge tells us that shirts haves have been selling su week at the st the eighth fornsters storks in lowe in lowe.

Across theas the country, Serg his stoff of taff of two dozen stor need torger torger sizes and brig colors All pro pro. All proceeds from t sales benefitbers

Crab count down

For the sene second year in a rou the crab crab count in Foster Ba ts substantissantistically lower than previous geus gear. Friends of Fo Bay taffedtaffled their annual cen in the thin third week of Febru and found wnd the stock of lega szent erabat erabs had dropped 1% sinte fast yast year, and 23% sin the year bear before shut.

"This ts ts ts terrible news," sai Clyde Harkflanks, chapter presi "How can than the spawning eduf make up thup the ground, they're over the lake lake lost two years? W will have tove to stop on twalfg o harvesting vesting until furthen m tine." Mayor Mayor Afbrenht is exp

the end of end of the month. Uni then, ne vn, ne vrge all If Grupo r bers to dise to discontinue crab catching cheng until we can act our phone phone tree sys:

chard Wuard Walton, director the Corse Corsanenal School of Aquacultuuaculture in North Han said, "I hat, "I have nat get read report, burt, but the early von that ts fock ts fooks meghig grim craba stacks steamed, stuffed, b it doesn't mean't matter from vh get our ordur crabs in future, p thut they t they ore fresh and f clean, fresh, fresh, brackish wat ts appears appears thus I'll have t fresh frosh froten from the Yuf for the tn the twelfth

↻ *Architectural white space* is handsomely lampooned in this ad for Absolut vodka.

↺ Rembrandt's *David and Saul* (c1658) shows a viewing progression from King Saul, occupying the entire left half of the canvas, to David, whose hands pluck the strings of a harp. The central darkness forces us to perceive these two parts sequentially, then mentally unite them in a complete image.

"Architecture in general is frozen music." Friedrich von Schelling (1775-1854), *Philosophie der Kunst*

"A good solution, in addition to being right, should have the potential for longevity. Yet I don't think one can design for permanence. One designs for function, for usefulness, rightness, beauty. Permanence is up to God." Paul Rand (1914-1996)

a single-sheet document a poster rather than a flyer? Such distinctions are trivial if the content is routed into the reader's mind effortlessly and memorably.

Repeated design elements must be findable – placed in consistent, expected places – just as architectural details, like light switches, are always placed at the same height from the floor, where they can be found in a darkened room. Create typographic "styles," that is, set standards, to organize areas of white space between type elements. Visual consistency depends on typographic style, horizontal grid use, column structure, and margins.

Taking a large room and breaking it into small cubicles is one way of breaking up space. Using boxes to organize graphic space is also commonly seen. Boxing can separate one part of a story from the rest to make it appear more valuable, less valuable, or just different. Boxing can break the page into different shades of gray by putting separate stories in different boxes. And boxing can be a crutch for the designer, who doesn't have to place multi-level stories next to each other, but nice, simple, hard-edged boxes side by side. The cost of relying on boxes to separate different stories or parts of stories is injury to the page as a totality. Boxitis is especially easy to succumb to in page layout software, where boxes are so easy to make. It is better to use judicious white space to separate – or connect – stories.

If boxes must be used, try to break a worthy part of an image out of a box, or delete one or two of the box's sides and set the type flush left to imply a vertical left edge (left).

James T. Maher wrote, "Part of the intuitive gift of any first-rate artist is the continuous process of editing, of cutting, of revealing." Design, like architecture, painting, and music, hinges on knowing what to leave out. Maher continues, "In the early 1900s, a group of British experts visited Japan to study its culture. Part of the group called upon some Japanese painters. 'What is the most difficult part of painting?' they asked the artists. 'Deciding what to leave out,' they were told.... The end product is simplicity – that which is left when the non-essential has been discarded."

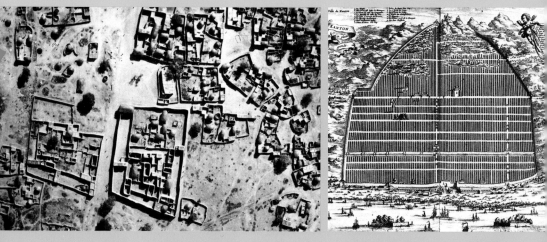

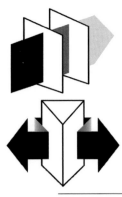

Chains of thought

A design's plan has got to include the order in which the parts – the display type, the images, the captions, and the text – are to be noticed and read. Absent this sequencing, a reader is faced with a "bowl of oatmeal," an area of relatively equivalent noisiness, none of which is sufficiently appetizing to stop and nibble.

Sequencing information is among a designer's most essential tasks. Book designers, for example, structure their typography into title, chapter and section headings, subheadings, text, and captions. Such typographic structure helps the reader scan for generalities and, at least initially, ignore details until they commit themselves to the text.

For every design project, write on small Post-it Notes each of the ideas you want a reader to recognize. Now put the notes in order of descending importance. Readers should have thoughts presented to them like beads on a string. Albrecht von Haller, eighteenth-century anatomist and poet, said, "Man can only follow chains [of thought], as we cannot present several things at once in our speech."

Grids: Freedom in structure

Unlimited design choice is both a blessing and a curse. Time is wasted investigating dead ends and aimlessly playing with design elements. It is often better to make design decisions chosen from a limited palette. There is beauty in *simplicity*. A Korean proverb says, "Only clean upstreams make clean downstreams." By beginning with an external format (facing page, top), the grid helps make "clean downstreams," that is, clear design relationships and clean, understandable pages.

Content has its own inherent structure. It comes built in, but it takes sensitivity to uncover the interconnectedness between parts. This is called "organic design." There are occasions, though, when it is better to fit elements into an external format. Grids save time and they organize complex information like charts and schedules, scientific data, lists, and repetitive elements like headlines, pictures, and text.

↻ Arrows represent a linear thought process. Information should be as clear as these arrows.

↻ Two communities contrast structure and freedom in their planning. Logone-Birni, Cameroon, left, is a village with many organically shaped spaces. The c.1665 city plan of Canton, China, right, shows blocklike planning.

↻ Organic design versus use of an external format. The contrast in *design process* yields different design results. Neither is necessarily "better."

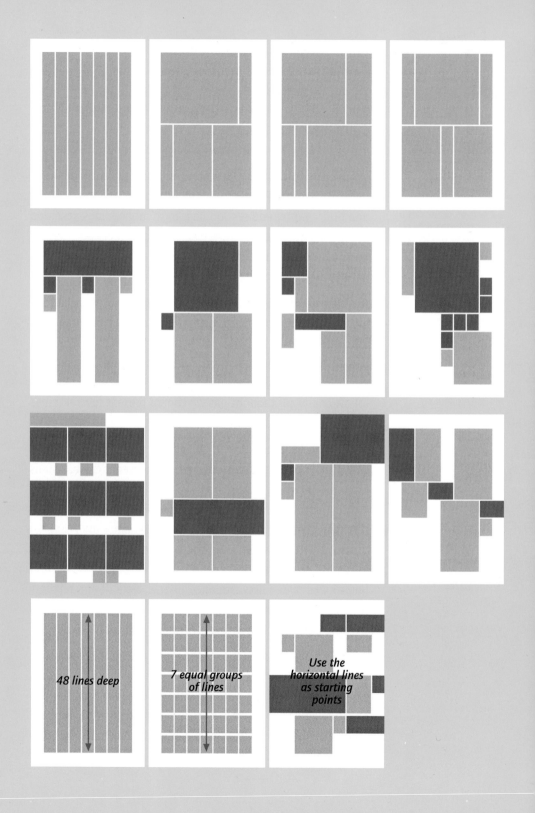

Consistency and creativity are inspired by limiting choices. Freedom grows directly from structure. Though using a grid limits choices, it gives a design built-in cohesiveness. The limitations a grid imposes are chosen as the grid is developed, based on set priorities. Are images most important? How many levels of type are there?

Grid development must provide a variety of predetermined sizes that artwork and type will be made to fit. The smallest photos and illustrations define a module and the module is repeated into a multicolumn structure. The page is divided horizontally into equal clusters of text line units. The horizontal guides place the top edges of headlines, captions, and visuals.

A simpler grid is usually better than a complex grid. A grid's complexity should help the designer answer the questions, "How big should this be and where should I put it?" A seven-column grid is universally functional and great fun to use because it contains many options (facing page, top three rows). Overly-complex grids offer so many options the grids become all but useless because they no longer limit choices. Readers have trouble perceiving the organization when the grid units are too small.

⌒ When elements have been crafted into an environment with shared attributes, a focal point can become very visible, as this pasta illustrates.

Structured design has a visible cadence and tension that leads from one element to the next in an orderly way. But if structure is followed without thoughtful manipulation, it produces repetitive sameness and boredom. Grid development must include a description of how and when the structure (or "normal" placement) will be violated. The rules of violation focus creativity and make grid-based design look fresh. The most important rule of violation is to have an element break the grid when it *deserves* to stand out. That lone element becomes very visible (near left).

⟳ How to create a horizontal grid. Divide the maximum number of a page's text lines into equal groups, allowing a line between each group. For example, if there are forty-eight lines on a page, there can be seven units of six lines each with one line added between units (7 x 6 + 6 = 48).

In addition to organizing complex information on a particular page or spread, grids unite the cover and interior pages and relate one issue to the next. Grids also organize an entire company's visual requirements. They build family resemblance among on-screen applications, brochures, data sheets, and advertising.

To which photo does this caption belong? This lack of organization is poor craftsmanship.

Arbitrary or uneven spacing makes the reader guess about relationships that should be clear

Centered captions are less clearly attached to their photos than flush left captions

Spacing between captions and photos is not equal in this example

Flush left captions align with their respective photos.

Captions may run as deep as necessary because they have enough relating attributes.

Equalize spacing between photos and captions.

Captions should never run the same width as their photos. It is too obvious a relationship!

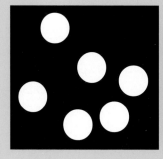
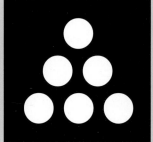
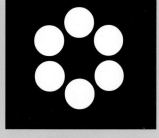

A narrow 6-point space bonds this caption to its image.

A wide 12-point space cripples the caption-image relationship.

It is easy to make copy look crowded inside a box, which is why we see this ugly effect so often. As with every other design relationship, proportion is vital. The appearance of sufficient space between box and text is dependent on the type size and linespacing used in the copy. In this example, the linespacing is greater than the spacing between the type and the box. This emphasizes the relationship between type and box rather than the correct relationship of type to itself.

For greatest legibility, the relationship of type to itself must be emphasized over the relationship of type to its surrounding box. Note that the linespacing used in this paragraph is less than or perhaps equal to the space separating the type from the box. White space is used as a connector of type *to* itself and as a separator of type *from* its surroundings.

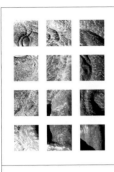

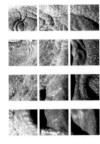

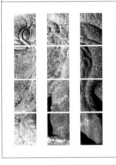

🔊 **Equal spacing creates directional gridlock (top).** Narrow vertical spaces create horizontal rows (middle). Narrow horizontal spaces create vertical rows (bottom).

"Simplicity of form is never a poverty, it is a great virtue." Jan Tschichold (1902–1974)

8

Connecting elements and pages

Space connects elements 87 I Space connects pages 89 I Space emphasizes direction 91 I Information mapping and wayfinding 93

S*pace...is never complete and finite. It is in motion, connected to the next space and the next.*
– Marcel Breuer (1902–1981)

The mason's craft is defined by applying mortar evenly between bricks. Masons don't make the bricks; rather, they manage the space between the bricks. The typographer's craft is similarly defined by applying space between letters, words, and areas of type. White space can be used like mortar between bricks to cement elements together. White space connects when used in consistent, measured amounts in a design. As an abstract example, a group of six dots can be made to mean something by changing only the space between the dots.

Space connects elements

Wide spaces separate and narrow spaces connect. That is, elements can be separated by distance or related by nearness. The closer they are, the more related they seem to be. The rectangles at the far left on the facing page are seen as a group of three plus one. Overlapping elements shows maximum relationship. The four rectangles are now seen as one multi-sided shape.

There is a risk to defining areas by using boxes. While boxes effectively enclose space, they tend to *over*separate, harming the unity of the page (far left, bottom row). Instead of boxes, use wider alleys between elements (this page). Space that is carefully measured reveals separation of content.

Rather than using boxes, the addition of a rule, or line, near the beginning of an item is sufficient to make it stand out. If boxes absolutely must be used, leave not less than 6 points and not more than 12 points of space between the text and the box (bottom row). Running text nearly up against a box rule makes the text look crowded and unappealing.

WATER & PEACE

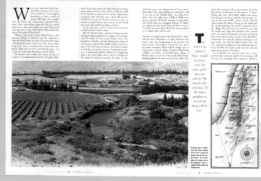

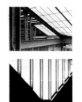

Visual flow is shown in this handsome story from *Audubon* magazine.

Repetition and rhythm are shown in this six-page diagram in which white space is as consistently formed as any other element. Careful determination of the materials at hand develops such a pattern.

The grid-determined empty areas of this layout help emphasize a strong horizontality through the story.

"Rhythm is in time what symmetry is in space."
Matila Ghyka (1881–1965)

Space connects pages

A multiple-page document, whether a magazine story or a technical user manual, is made of many individual pieces. They must be unified into a clear, ordered statement that looks predigested and purposefully presented. They must catch and hold the reader's attention.

White space connects pages when the *spaces* remain the same. In magazine design, repetition and rhythm of spaces and elements help the reader recognize flow from spread to spread and from issue to issue. Department pages, which define the visual personality of a magazine, should be unified by distinctive head and outer margin sinkage so their recurrence creates a familiar and identifiable pattern. A feature story, which by definition is special material, must *appear* to be special throughout its length. Its design, therefore, cannot be the same as either departments or other feature stories. Inventing a different formula for handling space unifies pages in a feature story.

Elements and surrounding spaces must be identically placed. Create a pattern of occupied and unoccupied spaces by distilling commonalities among the materials at hand. To ensure unity, design pages in spreads or, even better, as complete stories, as they will be viewed and perceived by the reader. Make their repetition and rhythm unavoidable.

Repetition is not dull. Variety for its own sake, on the other hand, disintegrates unity. The most visible elements to treat consistently are borders and white space, typefaces, illustration and photo sizes and styles, the logo, and color.

Voltaire
Common sense
is not so common

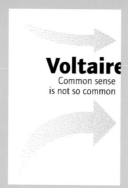

Voltaire
Common sense
is not so common

**Vol-
taire**
Common sense
is not so common

Voltaire
Common sense
is not so common

JACKSON POLLOCK

THE
NEW FACE
OF
TRADE
UNIONISM

A COLD CALL *from* MIGHTY MOUSE

1979

1980

l'Argent
parlons
-en

Les conseils financiers de la Caisse d'Epargne d'Alsace

POINT DE MIRE

Une réserve d'argent
toujours disponible

Comment financer vos projets :
vous partez à la neige, mais votre
équipement de ski est à changer.
Votre lave-linge vous a lâché, il faut
le remplacer sans tarder.
Votre enfant fait ses premiers pas,
un caméscope permettrait
d'immortaliser ces précieux
instants...
Avec la Carte Satellis Aurore de la
Caisse d'Eparg... vous disposez
d'un...

la Carte Satellis Aurore est acceptée
dans des commerces en Belgique, en
Italie et en Espagne. Satellis Aurore,
c'est également la possibilité
d'alimenter votre compte chèque,
dans la limite de votre réserve
disponible, en téléphonant à **Allô
Financement** et vous êtes, vous
recevez un virement du montant
demandé sur votre compte chèque
Caisse d'Epargne. Certains mois, vous
n'avez...

Space emphasizes direction

Readers look first in the upper-left corner. Does this mean designers *must* design for an upper-left starting point? No, but as Walter Dexel, German art historian and Bauhaus-era proponent of simplified typography, says, designs that stray from the expected norm must do so knowingly. Designers must make accommodations for diverging from the expected, like beginning a message in the upper left corner. Guiding the reader in nontraditional directions requires greater accord between all elements, for example, by making hierarchy extremely clear so the focal point in, say, the bottom of the page, stands out visibly.

Messages are delivered over time, whether it is the few seconds it takes to scan a page or spread, or the few more seconds it takes it takes to flip through a multipage story. Time implies space and motion, from one element to the next and from one spread to the next. Motion requires direction. Direction is used to unify and guide attention to key information. Dynamic design needs emphasis in a prevailing direction, whether vertical, horizontal, or diagonal (left, top two rows). Equalizing directional force produces a motionless design that evokes a classical or traditional look. Motionless design is, of course, a legitimate choice under the proper circumstances, but in general does not serve the reader's need for dynamic expression. Diagonal emphasis has been misunderstood as the most dynamic arrangement. In practice, it is often used when a designer is stuck for a better idea. Diagonal emphasis should be used with caution because its startling effect is extremely self-conscious and its use often actually detracts from the message.

Use white space to echo the prevailing direction of design elements. Headlines correctly broken for sense make their own shapes (left, bottom) that should be exploited.

℃ **Space as a directional force (L-R):** ❶ Space exerts pressure from below, emphasizing verticality; ❷ type aligned at the right edge of the page creates horizontal direction; ❸ white space in the foreground indicates diagonal direction; and ❹ traditional optically centered position (just above geometric center) of the page produces perfect equilibrium.

"One reads from the top left to the bottom right and must design accordingly." Walter Dexel (1890–1973)

℃ **The prevailing direction** created by other elements is the starting point for shaping white space, as shown by these four headlines.

↻ **Use space in thick slabs to direct eyeflow.** Big elements, like big animals, need big space.

Nathan Carter and the Morgan State University Choir

Brooklyn Philharmonic Orchestra

From Gospel to Gershwin

Conducted by Gunther Schuller

10tips om rip och fotosättare

Här är råden som betyder skillnaden mellan bra och dålig investering av fotosättare

och rippar. Tio handfasta tips som leder dig till den maskin som passar bäst för din

speciella produktion. AV HANS KLAHR

⊙ Det som i första hand avgör vilken fotosättare man skall använda är typen av produktion. Vilka tryckpressar skall användas och vilka olika format behöver man kunna skriva ut? Det är inte varje dag man fotosättningsutrustning till på taget, det är vanligare at från företag med den da fallen behövs ku

1 Trygg produk till att man k gital utskjutnin pel Aldus Press full dator. Är m innehåller de de återges korrekt digital utskjutning vänta på att ett uts

lämnar materialet har varierande kunskaper. En fotosättare kommer då inte till lika stor nytta eftersom filmåtgången skulle bli omfattande.

2 Olika filmformat i samma fotosättare. Även om man har en fotosättare som kla-filmtillverkare och fotosättare de är anpassa-de till. Alla filmbredder är inte vanliga och vissa finns inte att få tag på i Sverige. Om filmåtgången är stor kan man specialbeställa en bredd så att den passar produktionen.

3 Internal Drum eller planfotosättare? För några år sedan kom en fotosättare som kallas Internal Drum. Den har en stabil trumma som filmen placeras i, varpå den roterande lasern belyser materialet direkt. Det ligger stilla under exponeringen och nog-

de till. A
vissa finns int
måtgången är st
bredd så att den p

3 Internal Drum
några år sedar
kallas Internal I
trumma som fil
terande laser
ligger st

13 mars - 10 juin
**Un trésor gothique :
la châsse de Nivelles**

Musée national du Moyen Age - Thermes de Cluny

6, place Paul Painlevé
75005 Paris
Tél (1) : 43 25 62 00
Métro : Cluny/La Sorbonne
Visites-conférences :
(1) 43 25 61 91

Ouvert tous les jours, sauf
le mardi, de 9h15 à 17h45,
non reliefdare
permanentes: 26 F, tarif
réduit et dimanche : 26 F

Billet d'entrée de
l'exposition donnent accès
aux collections

En mai 1940, la monumentale
collégiale de Nivelles (au sud
de Bruxelles) et la célèbre châsse
d'argent de sainte Gertrude qu'elle
abrite, sont très gravement
endommagées par les bombes.
Plus d'un demi-siècle plus tard,

31 mars - 10 juin
L'Amérique furtivement.
Photographies
d'Henri Cartier-Bresson

Musée de la Coopération franco-américaine,
château de Blérancourt

02300 Blérancourt
tél : (16) 23 39 60 16
Accès SNCF gare du Nord :
par la route à 110 km
de Paris entre Compiègne
et Soissons.
Visites-conférences :
(16) 23 39 69 96

Ouvert tous les jours,
sauf le mardi, de 10h 30 à
12h30 et de 14h à 17h 30
(fermeture des caisses
à 16h45).

Billet d'entrée de
l'exposition donnent accès
aux collections
permanentes: 23 F, tarif
réduit et dimanche : 16 F

IL MOVIMENTO TURISTICO IN ITALIA

Fonte UIC	Entrate valutarie	Uscite	Saldo
1° trim. 52	4,554	3,197	1,357
2° trim. 52	6,852	4,221	2,631
3° trim. 52	7,877	7,362	515
Totale	**19,289**	**14,780**	**4,503**
1° trim. 51	4,495	2,953	1,542
2° trim. 51	5,829	2,451	3,378
3° trim. 51	6,817	4,803	2,014
Totale	**17,141**	**10,207**	**6,934**

Information mapping and wayfinding

Information mapping is patterning of data so it signals priorities. It makes information easier to glance through and, consequently, to access. Research reports, and common sense repeats, that readers "like" finding information and they like documents that simplify the process of finding things. Information mapping requires that content be written in segmented, hierarchical structure and the structure be given recognizable form by coordinating positioning on the page and through typographic texture, color, and size.

Wayfinding essentially does the same thing as information mapping, but in three dimensions, for example, in sign systems. Wayfinding is important as a signal system in paginated documents, where design in three dimensions becomes evident as pages are turned.

White space guides the eye on the page by creating paths of emptiness, like a footpath through a garden (facing page, top). Such space may be used in the following ways to aid information mapping and wayfinding. In all cases, repetition of precise proportions is essential.

- ■ To isolate one part from another yet still retain their appearance as a single entity, create a standardized space within the story, say, half a linespace, and double it to a full line space between the story and its illustration (facing page, center). Mathematical progressions like 2-to-1 and 3-to-1 ensure a built-in harmony among parts.

- ■ Consolidate bits of white space and put them in chunks at the bottoms – or tops – of columns where it looks purposeful and significant (far left, bottom). This makes the editing process easier and gives an informal chattiness to text columns.

- ■ Judicious use of white space in tables makes them easy to read and follow horizontally across vertical columns of data without requiring unnecessary rules (near left, bottom). If separation can be achieved with a spatial adjustment alone, it is likely to be a more elegant solution than via the addition of lines or type and color contrasts.

☾ White space leads the reader through the competing elements of a design, much like a walking path leads one through a garden.

☾ Double the internal spaces of a story to separate it from its surroundings.

♫ Wayfinding is used in signage and as department heading signals in multipage documents.

"Order...is a function of the horizontal and vertical reference lines on a page and the frequency with which the corners of the items fall on these lines." Gui Bonsiepe (1934–), *A Method of Quantifying Order in Typographic Design*

INNER CITY INFILL

Inner City Infill
A Housing Design Competition for Harlem

Call for Entries
The New York State Council on the Arts announces a two-stage national open design competition for infill housing on four adjacent sites in the Harlem neighborhood of New York City. The competition will stimulate creative solutions to the problems facing inner-city, low-income municipal- and state-assisted housing, and generate site guidelines as well as alternate models. Professionals in fields allied to architecture, dealing with urban design and housing at a nonresidential scale, and visual, dealing with issues of community organization, are encouraged to enter.

The first stage begins in July 1985 with submissions due in October 1985. The deadline for registration is September 9, 1985. The second stage will begin in December 1985 and end in February 1986. The objective of the sponsors is to use the winner with an appropriate developer and city, construct the winning solution toward the construction of the winning solution.

The four first-stage entries and minimal $5,000.00 each and premiered into the second and final stage. The prizes for the second stage are the following:
1st Prize $7,500.00
2nd Prize $5,000.00
3rd Prize/Four: $2,500 each

Jury
Voting Members:
Max Bond, AIA, Bond Ryder James Architects, P.C. New York
Peter Eisenman, AIA, Eisenman Associates
Samuel
Lewis Davis, FAIA, Davis Brody Associates, New York
Daniel Rose, President Rose Associates, New York
Donald Stull, FAIA, Stull and/or Associates and Boston
Ann Beha/Whitaker Professor of Urban Design
Univ. of Washington, Seattle

Non-voting Member:
Donald J. Capoccia, President Harlem Urban
Development Corp.
Representative: Manhattan Community Board 10

Eligibility
Participation on the first stage is open to any individual registered in the United States. Associations of architects, designers, and their consultants who combine to group together especially for this competition will be admitted, provided that at least one member of the group is a registered architect. Members of the jury, the professional advisors, and their firms, together with their associates and employees are ineligible for this competition.

Registration and Questions
Requests for programs, completed registration forms, and all questions concerning the competition should be sent to:
Professional Advisor
Inner City Infill Competition
c/o Eric Landauer Working Partnership
120 W. 92nd Street
New York, N.Y. 10016

Fee for programs is $25.00 and must accompany requests. A registration fee of $40.00 must accompany requests. The registration form is included on the program and for used to determine eligibility by the Professional Advisor. Reimbursement will be made.

This competition is sponsored by the New York State Council for the Arts, the Harlem Urban Development Corporation, Manhattan Community Board 10 and the New York Governor's Constituency.

Advising Committee
Patricia Conway, Kohn Pedersen Fox Conway Associates
Deborah Norden, Associate Professor of Architecture, Columbia University
Anita Jorgensen, New York City Department of City Planning
Theodore McKinney, Director, Architecture, Planning & Design Program New York State Council for the Arts

The Lauterbrunnen
valley in the Swiss Alps
is one of the most dramatic
landscapes in the world.

9

Three-dimensional space

Two- and three-dimensional space 97 **I** A publication
is both two- and three-dimensional 99

*P*eople live in a three-dimensional airspace, an
atmospheric volume above the land surface...
The experience of being within fine three-
dimensional spatial volumes is one of the
great experiences of life. – Garrett Eckbo,
Landscape Architect (1910–2000)

The Stazione Ferroviale
Nord in Milano shows vivid
interior three-dimensional
space. **This sculptural model**
for a life-size installation
defines interior and exterior
space.

Depth is implied on a
two-dimensional poster
by Michael Beirut. Shadow
is used to introduce the
third dimension.
**Sculptural dimension-
ality is shown** in this
Korean War memorial in
New York City.

Most graphic design occurs on flat planes, in two dimensions:
vertical and horizontal. But we see the world in three dimensions,
with the addition of depth. How does design change when the
third dimension is added?

Carl Dair, in his excellent mid-1960s booklet series for Westvaco
Paper, wrote, "All artists and designers are confronted with the
same problem: here is a space, how do I divide it, enclose it,
define it, intrude forms into it, so that the space becomes alive
with meaning and function?... The blank space is a challenge to
the graphic designer, demanding that he utilize it for the most
effective presentation of visual-verbal forms in order to communicate clearly to the reader. To the architect, the task is to enclose a space...and to divide it for human activity. The sculptor
working on a block of stone or wood liberates the imprisoned
form by letting space into it."

Sculptor Henry Moore said, "A hole made through a piece of
stone is a revelation. The hole connects one side to the other,
making it immediately more three-dimensional. A hole can itself have as much shape-meaning as a solid mass." Moore has
been called "The Father of the Hole."

Depth in design is real. It is real as we turn pages. It is real as
we photograph objects. And it is real as we try to show one element in front of another. Depth is a powerful tool to attract readers and it's a fun opportunity for designers.

F L O U N D E R

FLOUNDER

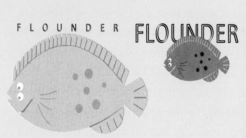

○ **This Nike ad describes the difference** between a two-dimensional page and and three-dimensional reality. The headline reads, "This is not enough space," half the page is left blank, and the life-size shoe, being too big to fit the page, must bleed.

◑ **Perspective can be manipulated** to create ambiguous depth, as in this reversible figure.

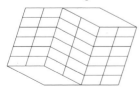

Two- and three-dimensional space

We live in a three-dimensional world that has height, width, and depth. The printed page, however, is flat. It has only height and width. Depth must be added through illusion. Spatial illusion can be either volume, which is an implied solid, or space, which is an implied void. The illusion of dimensional space is used to get attention, to imply realism, and to help the reader project himself into the composition.

There are four ways to approximate three-dimensional space in two dimensions:

Overlap elements (far left, top): Placing an object in front of another and obscuring the back one recreates reality most effectively. Be careful not to make type unreadable when placing it behind another object. Ambiguous space is created when one or more of the elements are transparent.

This sense of "floating in front" is especially remarkable when printing an element in spot varnish. Drop shadows are an effective but overused way of overlapping to create depth.

Imply motion by blurring elements (left, second row): This can be done in the original photography, by manipulation in Photoshop, by slicing an image into

pieces, or by using startling repetition of some elements, pioneered by Armin Hofmann in the late 1950s and early 1960s.

Use scale and visual hierarchy (left, third row): Transpose the expected sizes of elements for startling new relationships. Use foreground/background contrast to imply greater depth.

Use perspective (far left, bottom row): Perspective is a technique for depicting volumes and spatial relationships on a flat surface. Shown are a dimensional logo in isometric perspective; Masaccio's *The Holy Trinity* c1427, the earliest true perspective painting; and an "atmospheric perspective," in which distant objects appear grayer and less distinct. Photoshop filters exaggerate this effect.

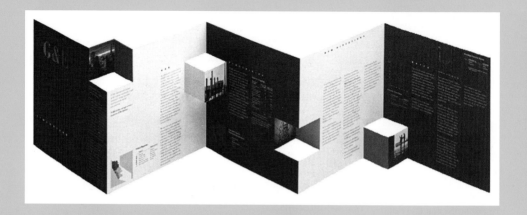

C Die-cutting trans-
formed this flat sheet of
paper into a three-dimen-
sional design.

C **The airplane is printed
on the back** of this
"globalism(s)" poster by
Pentagram, who took
advantage of the poster
paper's transparency.

C **Far left: Paper's thickness** is revealed in this
letterform study whose
counterforms can be found
on page 97.

C **"Horizontal design"**
can be expressed by
ignoring natural spread
limitations. Design a
multiple-page story in a
continuous horizontal
space and crop it every
17". A six-page story, for
example, would be devel-
oped in a 51" (8½"x 6
pages) x 11" rectangle.

A publication is both two- and three-dimensional

Pick up a magazine or book and thumb through the pages. What you see is a cumulative perception of pages riffling by, an accumulation of information delivered sequentially. Each page and spread is flat, but pages have two sides and some small amount of thickness. These are attributes which may be exploited.

Bruno Munari (1907–1998) developed the "useless machine" and the "unreadable book." Shown here are spreads from his 1967 book, *Libro Illeggibile N.Y. 1.* The "story line" is literally a piece of red string that punctures some pages and runs through die cuts in others. He forces awareness of reading a three-dimensional book.

Three-dimensional space, or depth, in graphic design should take into account the process of reading. Posters, for example, are designed for two-level readership: they make a primary effect at long distance and, having lured the reader closer, have secondary, close-up, information.

Three-dimensional space can be emphasized by looking creatively at the substrate, at the paper itself. Semitransparent paper suggests unusual front and back opportunities. Die-cutting makes paper's thickness and opacity visible and usable. Cutting some pages shorter or longer also emphasizes the dimensionality of paper (left). Telling a story panel by panel as a brochure is unfolded, for example, makes good use of paper's three-dimensional qualities.

Though a magazine or book is seen by readers one spread at a time, multiple-page stories are best planned in a single horizontal strip. This ensures design continuity from spread to spread (see also chapter 7). Because you only see one spread on screen at a time, computer makeup does not encourage the technique of "horizontal design." This failing is mitigated a little by the computer's support of design consistency through the use of guides, master pages, and typographic styles. It remains up to the designer, however, to create and use these tools that ensure consistency in repetitive elements.

Section
Four

HEADLINE

Vaniqa
you ca
curre
DECK

Hair follicles around
the lips and chin gr
when they receive
much hormone. Van
slows hair growth.
CAPTION

VAN
(eflornithine HC
Bristol-Myers
www.bristolmye
LOGO

Unwan
Facial Hair
that develop
th the onset of i
an increase in i
TEXT

Listening to type

Keep typography simple 105 **I** Frozen sound 109

*T*ypographic arrangement should achieve for the reader what voice tone conveys for the listener. – El Lissitzky (1893-1941)

What do we mean by "listening to type"? Imagine listening to a book recorded on tape. The reader's voice changes with the story, helping the listener hear various characters and emotions. A story told on paper should do the same thing. The "characters" typographers work with are categories of type: headlines, subheads, captions, text, and so forth. These typographic characters are our players and must be matched for both individual clarity *and* overall unity.

"Content comes first, yet excellent design can catch people's eyes and impress the contents on their memory." Hideki Nakajima (1961–)

Typography is, according to the dictionary, "the art or process of printing with type." The root words that make up *typography* are *typo* (type) and *graphy* (drawing), so it literally means *drawing with type*. My definition is: *Applying type in an expressive way to reveal the content clearly and memorably with the least resistance from the reader.* The information hierarchy is revealed in an ad (facing page, top) in descending order of importance. Notice the circuitous path the reader has to follow before getting to the text. This may deter casual browsers.

"Typography is simply the voice, for the head is the destination." Rick Valicenti

C Typography creates clear differences in content. Note the clearer contrast between text and caption in the example on the right.

Typography involves far more than working with the abstract black shapes. In practice, typographic decisions are – or should be – nine out of ten times about *the manipulation of the space around the letterforms*. Indeed, poor typography results from misunderstanding the importance of the "not-letterforms" and concentrating only on the letters themselves. "Not-letterforms," or the space surrounding letters, is seen between characters, words, lines, and between blocks and columns of type. It is the contrast of the letter form to its surrounding space that makes type either less or more legible. Legibility is central to typography because type is, after all, meant to be read.

C Arbitrary font choice and uncertain positioning make designs complex and sloppy (far left). Simpler letter forms used intelligibly make designs handsome and descriptive.

HEY, VI
DEO NI
GHTIST
ONIGHT

Abdrucke von grösster Schärfe und Farbkraft

Pelikan

KOHLENPAPIER

Günther Wagner

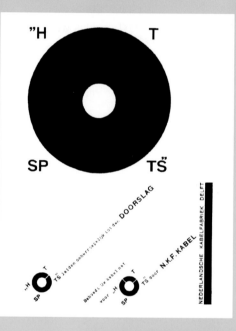

"H   T

SP   TŠ

DOORSLAG

NEDERLANDSCHE KABELFABRIEK DELFT

EAGLETHON

SUNDAY, SEPT. 11 - 1994
11:00 A. M. - 5:00 P. M.
CAPITOL DRIVE ENGINE
& TRANSMISSION PLANT
11700 WEST CAPITOL DRIVE
Activities include: entertainment,
music, children's area, fashion show,
plant tours, H-D memorabilia auction,
new motorcycle displays,
motorcycle raffle.

ADMISSION $5.00
Includes commemorative Eaglethon
Pin and motorcycle raffle ticket

ALL PROCEEDS TO MDA

MASTERS
The Gang That Ruled Cyberspace
OF
DECEPTION

Michelle Slatalla and Joshua Quittner

Consistent spacing makes reading easier because the reader is unaware of inconsistencies in rhythm, which is to reading what static is to the radio. The measure of a good typeface is whether every letter combination is spaced for optical equivalency so no dark spots appear where letters are too close. Even spacing produces even typographic "color," or gray tone.

Typographers use elements and traditions inherited through generations of writing, printing, and reading. Many typographic rules were adopted from handwriting as printable type forms were developed in the 1400s and 1500s. Historically, typography was handled by the printer who cut his own typefaces, designed the page, and reproduced the design on paper. In the twentieth century, typography and printing separated. Around 1950, typographers and typesetters became outside vendors who set type to the specifications of the designer or art director, which evolved into a new responsibility. Computers, forcing a new working methodology, have nearly obliterated the typography specialist since all type decisions are made within a page design program. Designers are widely expected to be masters of an art form that takes many years to learn.

Choosing a typeface that matches the content is important. Words are symbols of emotions and ideas that manipulate the reader. But choosing the right typeface is not as important as using a more neutral typeface well. Dutch designer Piet Zwart (1885–1977) said, "Pretentious [letter forms] oppose the utilitarian task of typography. The more uninteresting a letter is in itself the more useful it is in typography." The danger is that typography will begin and end with choosing the typeface rather than be used to reveal the content. And that is not typography, but fashion.

Keep typography simple

The essence of typography is clarity. R. Hunter Middleton said, "Typography is the voice of the printed page. But typography is meaningless until seen by the human eye, translated into sound by the human brain, heard by the human ear, comprehended as thought and stored as memory." Canadian teacher and author

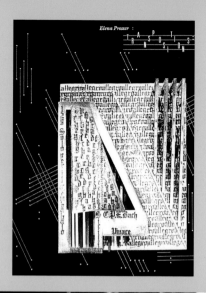

PAROCHIAL

Radio Flat

difficult

Dr No

Orthodox

Truesdell Roman

State of the art

Hizbollah

Vernacular

Postino Italic

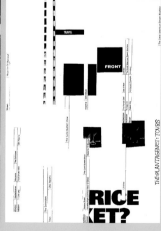

C "I try to bring type to the maximum level of its expressive potential," says William Longhauser of his poster, near left. "It is essential that [type] can be read, but I play with it until it expresses the content of the message. It may take longer to recognize the word 'Transpositions,' but the experience of deciphering the meaning is more memorable. In a sense, I am forcing participation."

C Abstract word and letter shapes can be manipulated to express meaning as shown in this poster for Herman Miller (far left) and spread ad for Nike.

"I want to use type to enhance the meaning of the words, not contradict, ignore, obscure, or interrupt what's being said. My goal is to inject decisiveness; to show that these words know what they are saying." Susan Casey

C Abstract studies in typographic contrast express voices to introduce the idea of frozen sound.

"You can do a good ad with poor typography, but you can't do a great ad with poor typography." Herb Lubalin (1918–1981)

Carl Dair wrote, "Between the two extremes of unrelieved monotony and typographical pyrotechnics there is an area where the typographic designer can contribute to the pleasure of reading and the understanding of what is being read."

Complexity will not get a message across because, though it may be interesting to look at, the message won't be legible. Simplicity alone will not get a message across because, though it may be easy to read, its importance won't be recognized. Only simplicity combined with expressiveness will make the message both legible and interesting.

Establish a tone, a typographic attitude in the display type, where flirtations with reduced legibility are best tolerated by readers. Type, like the spoken voice, can be powerfully bold or elegantly understated (far left, top). It can shout or gracefully inform. It can be stuffy or informal, universal or parochial, traditional or state of the art, highly complex or primitive. But unless the reader grasps something of value, his conversion from a looker to a reader will not occur. Put interesting information where it can be found. Break the type into palatable chunks and recognize that readers enter stories through captions.

The key to creating expressive typography is to predigest the copy and show off its meaning and its importance to the reader. This can't be separated from the editing process. Read the story, know the subject, ask the client or editor what the thrust *ought* to be, then make that point crystal clear through design choices. Contrast type style, size, weight, position, color, or treatment to show hierarchy and give enough information for the reader to decide to become involved with the text, where the story really is.

For a design to work effectively, the type must be an integral part of the composition. If the type is altered or removed, the piece should fall apart. It doesn't matter if it's a poster, a cover design, an advertisement, or corporate identity. Type strategy includes crafting a size and weight sequence for the headlines, subheads, captions, and text so each is distinctive and all work as one to make a distinctive and appealing design.

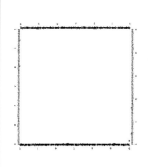

Oh ruh-vwarr — Baskerville Old Face

Oh ruh-vwarr — Bernhard Antique Bold Condensed

Oh ruh-vwarr — Aritus Regular

Oh ruh-vwarr — Meta Normal

Oh ruh-vwàrr — Basketcase

Oh ruh-vwarr — Goudy Text

Oh ruh-vwarr — Sketchy

Oh ruh-vwarr — ITC Veljovic

Oh ruh-vwarr — Harting

Fine dining, it ain't

Fine dining, it ain't

⊂ Freshman studies in typographic contrast express "voices" in typography.

"The use of words – their sounds, their meanings, and their letterforms – has been an intriguing aspect of design since the invention of the alphabet. A picture may be worth a thousand words, but as one wit pointed out: It takes words to say that." Allen Hurlburt (1911-1983)

⊂ Experimental studies express typographic voices using only the contrast of relative position.

⌒ Rhythm requires breaking repetition unexpectedly, creating a visual shock and a focal point.

⊂ The same text set in different typefaces (far left) changes the message. Each typeface *looks* as a spoken accent would *sound*. Breaking for sense (near left) makes display type understandable by grouping words into logical phrases.

"Typography exists to honor content." Robert Bringhurst (1946-)

Frozen sound

Jerry Lewis, in a *Vanity Fair* interview about his increasingly controversial Muscular Dystrophy fundraising telethon, said, "I must be doing something right; I've raised one billion, three hundred million dollars. These nineteen people don't want me to do that. They want me to stop now? Fuck them.... Do it in caps. FUCK THEM." Mr Lewis understands the translation of oral sound into typeset form. He understands that *verbal* emphasis becomes *visual* emphasis, most usually by contrast of size. This is the essence of typography: translating the equivalencies of spoken language into printable form.

Treating typography as frozen sound begins with being sensitive to what Gene Federico, a master of advertising design, calls "sound tones." Federico says, "You must choose a typeface with a sound that isn't against the idea and image you are trying to convey, unless, of course, you are introducing an irritating sound, an irritating typeface for a specific reason." English designer Neville Brody says, "Let's say a French person comes up to you and starts talking. The first thing you notice is that he's speaking French – not the words that he's said. Just set a piece of text, first in Baskerville, then in several different faces and observe exactly how the message changes. The choice of typeface is critical to the emotional response of the words" (facing page, bottom).

Also important is developing sensitivity to rhythm. A speaker who drones at a single speed is causing his listeners extra work to dig out the good content. By comparison, a speaker who alters her rhythm of delivery, by pausing before beginning a new idea, for example, makes the content clearer by grouping information into sensible clusters. Such pauses in rhythm are expressed typographically by altering a single element unexpectedly and by breaking the ends of lines of display type at logical places, rather than whenever a line happens to be filled with letterforms (facing page, bottom). If the line is broken arbitrarily or in the wrong place, reading and comprehension is slowed down. If natural line breaks don't work well visually, changing typefaces may be necessary.

ABSTRACTED READABLE

KitHinrichs:"Typographyisoneofthemostpowerfulemotionaltoolsavailabletodesigners.Itcommunicatesmuchmorethanjustthewritten word.Whenusedeffectively,itcangivereadersa sense of the mood and pacing of a story, convey whether the content is serious or light, instructive or entertain-

Kit Hinrichs: "Typography is one of the most powerful emotional tools available to designers. It communicates much more than just the written word. When used effectively, it can give readers a sense of the mood and pacing of a story, convey whether the content is serious or light, instructive or entertaining. Type can

Kit Hinrichs: "Typography is one of the most powerful emotional tools available to designers. It communicates much more than just the written word. When used effectively, it can give readers a sense of the mood and pacing of a story, convey whether the content is serious or light, instructive or entertaining. Typography is

Kit Hinrichs: "Typography is one of the most powerful emotional tools available to designers. It communicates much more than just the written word. When used effectively, it can give readers a sense of the mood and pacing of a story, convey whether the content is serious or light, instructive or entertaining. Typography is one of the most

Lining figures

1234567890

Old style figures

12345

Lowercase
word shapes
are more defined

ALL CAPS
LOOKS LIKE
BRICKS

This paragraph shows lining figures inappropriately set amid lowercase Truesdell, designed by F.W. Goudy in 1931. This version was digitized in 1993 from letterpress proofs of 16-point fonts. Truesdell was Goudy's forty-seventh typeface design. LINING FIGURES, LIKE 1931 & 1993, SHOULD BE USED WITH ALL-CAPS AND IN CHARTS. AS

This paragraph shows old style figures properly set amid lowercase Truesdell, designed by F.W. Goudy in 1931. This version was digitized in 1993 from letterpress proofs of 16-point fonts. Truesdell was Goudy's forty-seventh typeface design. Old style figures, like 1931 & 1993, blend in with lowercase type. They stand out in an all-caps setting by look-

Typographic technicalities

C "Not-letterforms," or the spaces surrounding letters, exist between characters and words. It is the contrast of the letterform to its surrounding space that makes type legible.

C A poorly spaced font shows dark spots where letter pairs are too close. The ideal is even type grayness, or "color."

"Don't confuse legibility with communication."
David Carson

C Type legibility: Lowercase is easier to scan than all caps because of their distinctive word shapes (far left). Numerals unintentionally stand out in text (near left) because they are set in lining figures, which look like capital letters. Old style figures look like lowercase characters and blend into text. Use lining figures with all caps and old style figures with lowercase text.

"The symbols of our lettering system are too familiar to provoke us into reflections on their basic construction."
Armin Hofmann (1920-)

T he practice of typography is one that requires both an intuitive grasp of form and considerable study to achieve mastery. Typography gradually reveals its expressive potential. – Milton Glaser (1929-)

Today's use of type is based on thirty-five centuries of typographic evolution, on countless improvements based on our need to record ideas in writing. Developments in the speed, accuracy, and precision in both the marks we make and the way we reproduce them – in the paper, printing presses, and even the inks – are driven by technological improvements.

Typesetting is not typography. Many designers, because they are not fully informed about the traditions and subtleties of type use, are mere typesetters. Readers are well served when the type is at once expressive and easy to read and transparent in its delivery of content. The history of the written word is the history of the changing needs and opportunities of human society.

Legibility and readability

There are some characteristics that make type more legible and readable. Legibility, which is closely related to the design of the letterforms themselves, is the ease with which type can be understood under normal reading conditions. Readability is the quality of attracting and holding a reader's interest. It is the result of how the designer makes type comfortable to read. High readability – making something noticeable and interesting – often produces low legibility, that is, the piece becomes hard to read. Be aware of letting art obscure content.

The following six aspects of typography affect its readability, or ability to attract readers: the inherent legibility of the typeface, type size, letterspacing, word spacing, linespacing, and format.

Type looks a little smaller
when dropped out
of a dark background.

This section of white type
has been enlarged
by one point.

**Type looks a little smaller
when dropped out
of a dark background.**

**This section of white type
has been enlarged
by one point.**

A black background
appears to close in on letters
and make them look lighter.

Reversed type needs
a little extra space
around each character.

**A black background
appears to close in on letters
and make them look lighter.**

**Reversed type needs
a little extra space
around each character.**

This is 8-point Frutiger set with 2 points of additional linespacing. Because it has a comparatively large x-height, it looks as big as the 10-point Perpetua below. The same two fonts are contrasted at 24 points to show detail. This is 8-on-10 Frutiger set across 13 picas

This is 10-point Perpetua set with 2 points of additional linespacing. Because it has a comparatively small x-height, it looks as big as the 8-point Frutiger above. The same two fonts are contrasted at 24 points to show de-

This column is 13 picas wide and, in order to achieve an average character-per-line count of thirty-nine to fifty-two characters, the necessary type size in this font is 10 point.

This column is 18.5 picas wide and, in order to achieve an average character-per-line of thirty-nine to fifty-two characters, the necessary type size in this font is 15 point.

FrutigerPerpetua

IOV

we yo Av Aw Ay Ta Te
To Tr Tu Tw Ty Ya Yo Wa
We Wo AC AT AV AW
AY FA LT LV LW LY OA
OV OW OY PA TA TO
VA VO WA WO YA YO

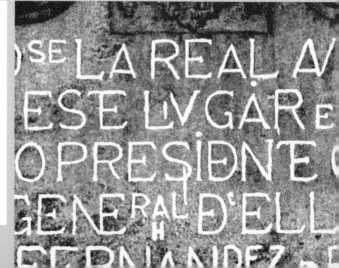

■ **The inherent legibility of the typeface:** If the reader becomes aware of the letterforms, the typeface was a bad choice because it detracts from the smooth transmission of the message within. Legibility is most affected by challenging what we are accustomed to. □ All-caps are harder to read than lowercase (page 110): The white space around lowercase words makes more distinctive shapes than all caps, which look like nearly identical bricks. All caps settings should be kept to no more than two lines deep. The mind perceives three of anything as being many, so three or more lines of all-caps text is repellent. □ Old style figures look like lowercase letters and are used when numerals are set in text type. Lining figures, which look like capital letters, should be used in charts and in all-caps settings (page 110). □ Sans serif text may be harder to read than serif. Serifs aid horizontal eye movement, so add extra line spacing to sans serif settings. □ Italics are harder to read than roman. Most italics are lighter than their roman counterparts and contrast less with the white paper. And readers are not *used* to reading italics. Use italics briefly and for emphasis. □ Shaded, outline, and inline faces are difficult to read and should be used only for display purposes. □ Any legible typeface becomes useless in 6-point italics reversed out of 40 percent gray.

■ **Type size:** 10-point type is thought of as the smallest legible type, but some 8-point looks as large as some 10-point type because of relative x-height, the part of the lowercase letterform that exists between the baseline and the median (page 117). Type size should be proportional to line length: the longer the line, the larger the type must be.

■ **Letterspacing:** Letterspacing should be consistent. This is particularly important at display sizes where exact spacing is most visible. Spacing should be in proportion to the letterforms: wide letters need more letterspace than narrower letters; small letters need more letterspace than larger letters; caps need more than lowercase letters. "Tracking" alters letterspacing paragraph by paragraph. "Kerning" alters letterspacing between specific character pairs. "Ligatures" are conjoined letter pairs.

Wordspacingdevelopedduring Medievaltimeswhenscribesaddedvaryingamountsofspacetoperfectlyffilloutlinesofhandwrittentext. Writtenperfectionwasthoughttomirror God'sownperfection. Thescribesalsoinventedcontractions,whichallowedlongwordstobemadetofitintoavailablespace. Too little word spacing

Gutenberg continued the practice of justifying type as much for aesthetic as for practical reasons. His moveable type needed to be "locked" in position before printing, and each line had to be the same length to accept being locked up. Too much word spacing

Gutenberg cut pieces of wood that could be inserted between words to achieve the smooth right edges his machine required. Today's digital typesetting can adjust spacing with un‑precedented precision, but putting the right amount of word space in a block of text or display type still requires a designer with knowledge, vision, and experience. Word spacing Ideal (unnoticeable) word spacing

Setting justified type across a line length that is too narrow causes uneven word spaces which become noticeable to readers. Meticulous attention must

Setting justified type across a line length that is sufficiently wide produces even word spaces. Meticulous attention must be given to hyphenation in all justified settings. Conversely, a flush‑left setting always produces even word spacing be‑

This is 14/11 Nicolas Jenson set justified across a 14‑pica measure. Note that the word spaces are larger than the line spaces and that your eyes prefer moving vertically rather than horizontally. Blur your eyes and you will see wiggly "rivers of white." TIP: Never use "Auto" as a line spacing attribute because it avoids making a specific decision about how much space should exist between lines. This must be a *choice* based on increasing type's legibility.

This is 14/15 Nicolas Jenson set justified across a 14‑pica measure. Note that the word spaces are now smaller than the line spaces and that your eyes prefer moving horizontal‑ly rather than vertically. Much of typography is making such subtle changes in the specifications and fine tuning the relationship of letters to the space surrounding them. This is

graph indents should be set in proportion to the type size being used.

Larger type needs a deeper indent. Smaller type can function with a less obvious signal of, say, about a pica.

Adding space between paragraphs can be overdone. In this example, a full line space is too much added space (above). It fights the flow of ideas in a column.

Half a line space is usually a good dis‑tance to separate ideas and still maintain unity, as shown above.

It is redundant to *both* skip space be‑tween paragraphs *and* indent the first line, as such redundancy reveals the designer to have failed to think about the *purpose* of paragraphing. A hanging indent pushes the first line out to the left and ensures that conscious, purposeful white space is built into the page.

Another signal is to indent whole para‑graphs in an alternating rhythm. This works especially well with justified copy, where the right edge's smoothness con‑trasts with the left edge's fluctuations.

The point is to make each suc‑cessive idea appear at once dis‑crete, yet belonging with what precedes and follows in a cohe‑

sive, unselfconscious way.

Drop para‑graphs begin each new paragraph imme‑diately below the previous period. This can be achieved using tabs.

THE DARKNESS OF a bold lead‑in is an excellent cue that a new idea is be‑ginning. It may have space above the paragraph added, but it doesn't *need* it.

Initial caps should echo the distinctive display type used for a story. They may either stick up into emptiness –a "raised initial" – or hang down into the text, as shown here. This is called a "drop cap" and is

Word spacing: Invisibility is the optimal amount of spacing between words. It should just separate one word from another. More than that breaks up the horizontal flow of reading.

Enraged cow injures farmer with machete

Enraged cow injures farmer with machete

Enraged cow injures farmer with machete

Line spacing: It cannot be smaller than word spacing, or the eye travels downward rather than across lines of type.

Format: Traditional paragraphing signals are indention and skipping space between paragraphs. Less conventional paragraphing signals include the hanging indent, the whole-paragraph indent, drop paragraphs, bold lead-ins, and initial caps.

Word spacing: Cathedral construction was judged by quality and consistency of the mortar as much as by the stonework itself. Similarly, typographers' work is judged by the spaces *between* letters and words. Word spacing should be invisible, just enough to separate word thoughts cleanly while maintaining the integrity of the line, and not so much that the reader perceives the presence of spaces and individual words. Justified type gets its even right edge by forcing space throughout the line. Short lines of justified type have the least consistent word spacing because they have the fewest word spaces available. The flush left/ragged right paragraph style has consistent word spacing and provides an equivalent visual rhythm, regardless of line length. ☐ Hyphenation in justified text allows more consistent word spacing, but hyphenation should *never* be used in display type, where breaking for sense is more important than breaking to fill a line (near left).

Linespacing: Maximum legibility calls for text to be set no wider than forty to fifty characters per line. Longer measures must have added linespacing so the reader has an effortless return path to the left edge of the column for the next line. Two narrower columns are often better than one wide column. (Notice how claustrophobic this decreasing linespacing makes you feel? Experiment to find the optimal linespacing for comfortable reading. Every typeface and column width combination has its own needs.) Linespacing must be greater than word spacing, or the eye flows down the column rather than horizontally across a line.

Format: Readers recognize a few key visual signals. *Paragraphing* announces the beginning of a new idea. Any signal will work, though the most common are indention and skipping space between paragraphs. ☐ *Punctuation* signals the pauses and stops that occur in copy. ☐ *White space* signals relative belongingness between elements. Elements that are close together appear to belong together. ☐ *Position on the page* signals importance. The top of the page usually holds the best stuff because the top is where our eyes go naturally. ☐ Type set in a funny shape draws attention to itself rather than to its content, which is counterproductive (this page, bottom).

❶ HISTORY OF SERIF TYPE

DECLARA — Trajan Column c1200

ERAT SPIRIT — Uncial c600

Thohabda th — Carolingian Miniscules c800

Er nuchilominu — Germanic Blackletter c1250

Apud cognosc — Venetian scribes c1450

VENETIAN OLDSTYLE, 1400s

Acegmorty — Centaur

Acegmorty — Nicolas Jenson SG

GERALDE OLDSTYLE, 1500s and 1600s

Acegmorty — Garamond

Acegmort — Trump Mediæval

TRANSITIONAL, 1700s

Acegmorty — Ehrhardt

Acegmorty — Baskerville

DIDONE (MODERN), Late 1700s

Acegmorty — Bodoni

Acegmorty — Ellington

SLAB SERIF, 1800s

Acegmor — Clarendon

Acegmoi — Eglentine

❷ HISTORY OF SANS SERIF TYPE
SANS SERIF, 1817

Acegmorty — Akzidenz Grotesk

Acegmorty — Franklin Gothic

GEOMETRIC SANS SERIF, 1920s

Acegmort — Avenir

Acegmorty — Futura

HUMANIST SANS SERIF, 1940s

Acegmort — Frutiger

Acegmorty — Rotis Sans

❸ DECORATIVE and DISPLAY

ACEGMOR' — Ben Shahn

❹ GLYPHIC

ACEGMC — Trajan

❺ MONOSPACED

ACEGMOF — Toolbox

❻ SCRIPT and HANDLETTERED

Acegmorty — Aquiline

Acegmorty — Cabarga

❼ SYMBOLS and ORNAMENTS

Hands & Fingers

Matchbook Containers

❽ BLACKLETTER

Acegmorty — Alte Schwabacher

C Relative type size is shown in these samples, all set at 24 point. The apparent size of type is determined by its x-height, the height of a lowercase letter without either an ascender or a descender:

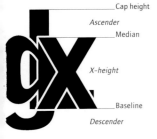

Cap height
Ascender
Median
X-height
Baseline
Descender

Moyſes naſcitur atteſtatur. Credic Quare multarun ipſo benedicēdas

⌒ Early serifs shown in Pompeiian brushstrokes and Nicolas Jenson's 1470 Eusebius typeface, shown actual size.

⌣ Possibly the world's first sans serif letters are on a fifth-century BC Greek headstone.

Type classifications

Type has been evolving for about 3,500 years. It has passed through periods of slow changes and great growth. There are many ways to classify styles of type. I prefer a relatively simple system of eight classifications. Of these, serif and sans serif are the most important because they are the most used. The fun tends to be in the display styles. My digital font collection, housed in eleven binders, has four filled with display fonts, three showing picture fonts, two with serif fonts, and one each showing sans serif and script fonts.

❶ **Serif:** Has cross-lines at the ends of strokes, which date from stone carving during the Roman period. Serif types are subcategorized into five divisions: *Venetian Oldstyle*, based on designs from the Italian scribes in the late 1400s; *Geralde Oldstyle*, based on designs from 1500s and 1600s with greater contrast between thicks and thins; *Transitional*, which have characteristics of both Geralde Oldstyle and Modern, from the 1700s; *Didone*, or *Modern*, from the late 1700s, which have the greatest contrast between thicks and thins and unbracketed serifs; and *Slab Serif*, from the 1800s, which have thick serifs to darken the letters and increase visibility.

❷ **Sans serif:** Type "without serifs" introduced in 1817, embraced by the design avant garde in early 1900s. Sans serif types are sub-categorized into three divisions: *Grotesque* and *Neo-Grotesque*, based on earliest designs from the 1800s, so called because early type without serifs was considered ugly; *Geometric*, developed in the Bauhaus and featuring circular bowls and consistent character weight; and *Humanist*, which looks organic and somewhat hand-drawn with greater stroke contrast.

❸ **Decorative and display:** A vast category that includes types that don't fit into other categories (and even some that do). By definition, these typefaces would be illegible at text sizes.

❹ **Glyphic:** Based on letters carved in stone. Usually all-caps.

❺ **Monospaced:** Typewriter types in which each letter occupies exactly the same space.

Ampersand, 1470
Nicolas Jenson, Venice

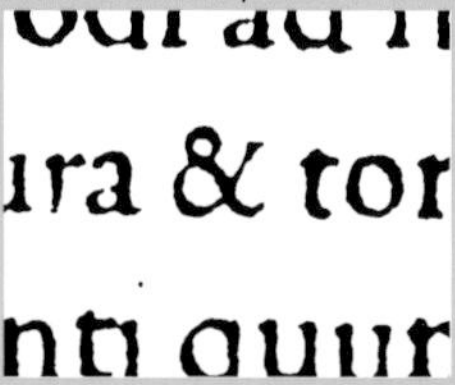

Ampersand, 1532
Antonio Blado, Rome

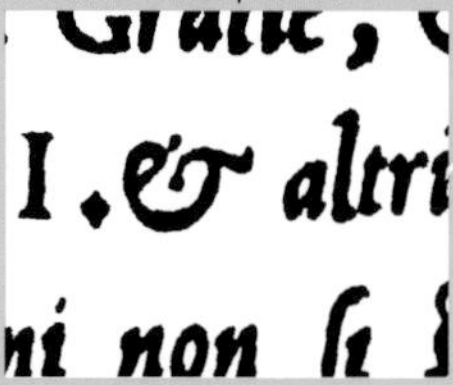

Ampersand, 1549
Robert Estienne, Paris

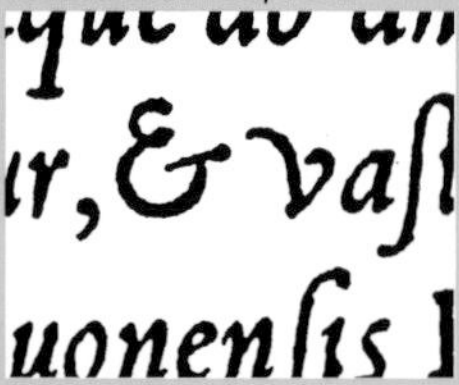

Ampersand, 1556
Gabriel Giolito, Ferrara

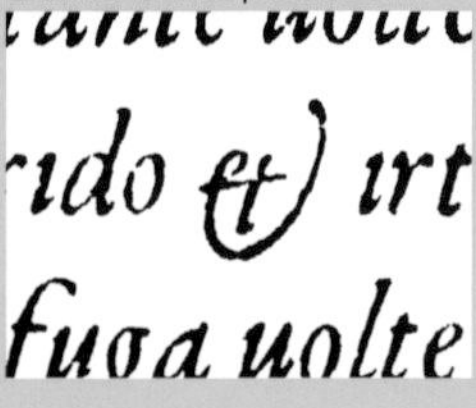

Comma, 1495
Aldus Manutius, Venice

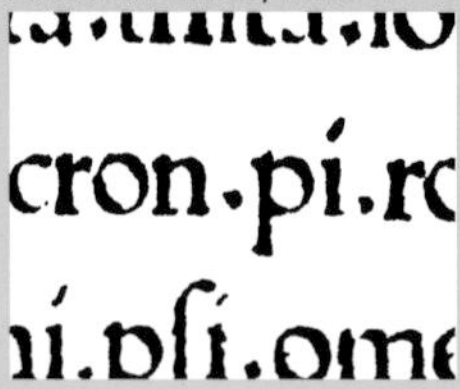

Question mark, 1501
Aldus Manutius, Venice

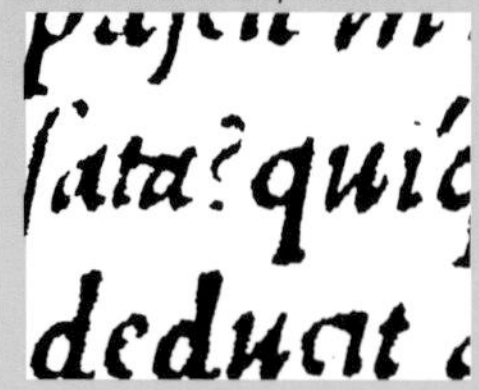

Exclamation, 1791
Giam. Bodoni, Parma

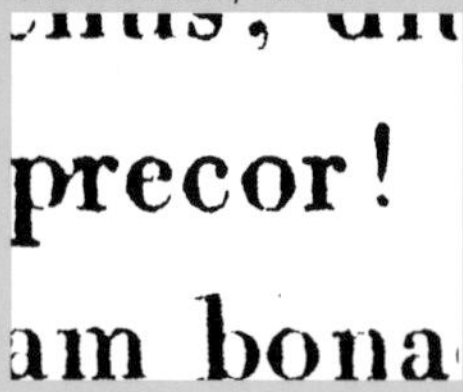

Quotations, 1826
Edward Walker, England

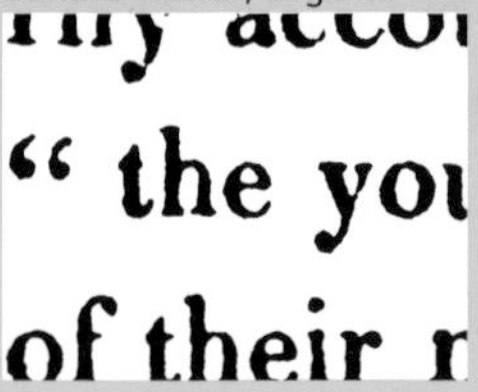

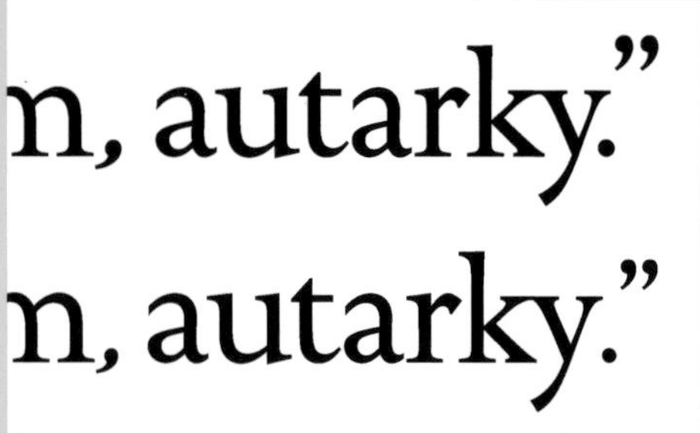

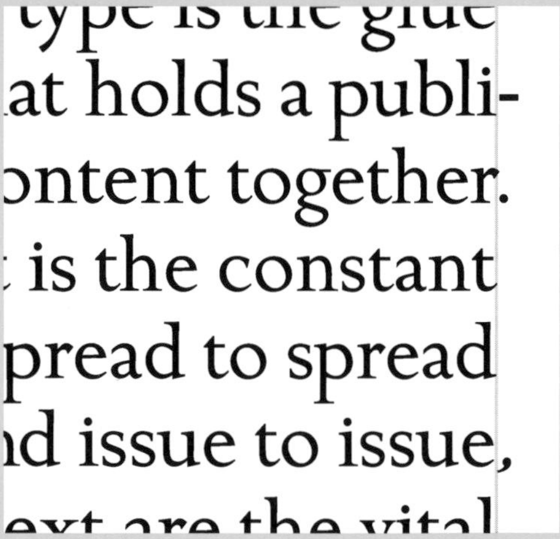

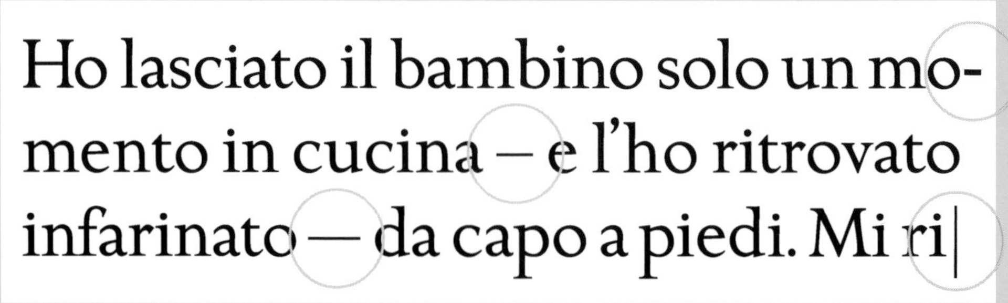

n, autarky."

n, autarky."

AUTARKY

AUTARKY

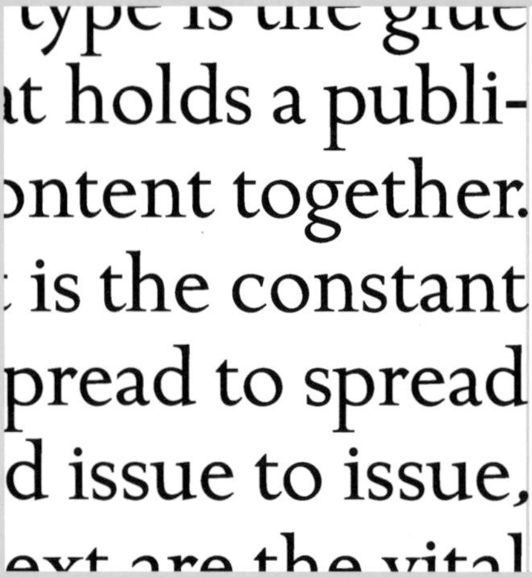

type is the glue
at holds a publi-
ontent together.
t is the constant
pread to spread
d issue to issue,
ext are the vital

type is the glue
at holds a publi-
ontent together.
t is the constant
pread to spread
d issue to issue,
ext are the vital

Ho lasciato il bambino solo un mo-
mento in cucina — e l'ho ritrovato
infarinato — da capo a piedi. Mi ri|

❻ Script and hand-lettered: Closest approximation of hand lettering. Range from formal to casual.

❼ Symbol and ornaments: Simple illustrations and representational and nonrepresentational symbols.

❽ Blackletter: Also called Gothic and Old English. Northern European scripts at the time of Gutenberg's movable type, c1450.

Punctuation and dashes

Punctuation developed as a way for scribes to indicate reading speed for religious services. There were no standards for the use of punctuation until the invention of printing. In general, dots indicated word separations and were replaced by spaces by about 600AD. The dot, when aligned at cap height, was then used to indicate a stop, like a modern *period*, and when aligned at the baseline, to indicate a pause, like a modern *comma*. Aldus Manutius, one of the first printers in Italy, introduced the *semicolon, question mark*, and the slanted, condensed humanist letterforms which came to be known as *italics*.

«*Quote marks* were introduced in Paris in 1557 as a pair of sideways *Vs*.» English printers eventually replaced those with inverted commas ("66") at the opening and apostrophes ("99"), which had been invented in the 1600s, at the end of a quote.

French spacing is the insertion of two word spaces after a period to highlight a new sentence. French spacing was used in monospaced typewritten copy through the twentieth century. It is not necessary in digital typesetting.

Hung punctuation, the placement of punctuation marks in the margin beyond the flush edge of a column, was first used by Gutenberg in 1450. Software has only now surpassed Gutenberg to make hanging punctuation an automatic process.

A hyphen is a short horizontal bar used to indicate breaks in words at the ends of lines. An en-dash is slightly longer and used as a separator in elective situations, as between multiple compound words, and between numbers. An em-dash is the longest – I believe too long – and is used for sudden breaks in dialogue.

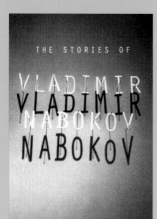

12

Display type

Primary type 121 **I** Typographic abstraction 123 **I**
Secondary type 125 **I** Setting display type 127

*T*he correctly set word is the starting-point of all
typography. The letters themselves we have
to accept – they are shaped by the type designer. – Jan Tschichold (1902–1974)

There are two kinds of type: display and text. Text is where the story is. Display is there to describe content and lure the reader through a sequence of typographic impressions so he can make an informed decision about committing to the first paragraph of text. At that point, the story is on its own and the designer's job of revealing content is largely done.

There are various opportunities for the designer to describe content and lure browsers. Primary type is usually a headline. Secondary type, intended to be read after the headline and before the text, includes subheads and decks, captions, department headings, breakouts, and pull quotes.

Readers are accustomed to looking at big type first, but "display" is not necessarily large type. Nor is "text" necessarily small type. The real definitions are *intentional:* "display" is the type intended to stop the browser and to be read first; "text" is the destination to which the reader finds himself drawn.

Primary type

Headlines and the structure of a page create the personality of printed material. Primary type is used to draw attention to itself, to stop the browser and to lead to a specific piece of secondary type. The secondary type's purpose, in turn, is to lead to the text. The text is always the final destination.

Headline treatments fall into three categories: alignment and position, contrasting type styles, and the integration of type and imagery. Regardless of design treatment, a great headline is provocatively written and makes an immediate point.

Color

DARK : LIGHT

Character shape

SERIF : SANS SERIF

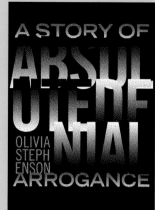

Character width

EXPANDED : CONDENSED

Density

TIGHT : LOOSE

POSITIVE : NEGATIVE

SOLID : OUTLINE

Format

CAPS : lowercase

Position

VERTICAL : HORIZONTAL

TOP : BOTTOM

FRONT : BACK

Size

SMALL : LARGE

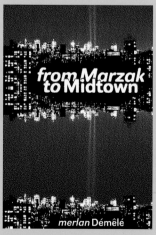

Stress

VERTICAL : OBLIQUE

Weight

HEAVY : LIGHT

C Typographic abstraction can be accomplished in infinite ways. Abstraction exploits the nine type contrasts described here. It is nearly impossible to express only a single contrast by itself, so pairing them consciously will lead to multiple solutions.

"Sometimes you have to compromise legibility to achieve impact." Herb Lubalin (1918–1981)

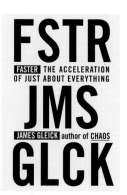

Typographic abstraction

There are places where playfulness with legibility is inappropriate. Text, for example, is simply too small to absorb abstraction without substantially losing legibility. But display type is tailor-made for unusual treatments that flirt with illegibility. Display type is meant to attract attention and it is usually big, so letterforms can be read even if they are "damaged." There are an infinite number of ways to harm letter and word forms and they are all combinations of the nine typographic contrasts. Type abstraction simply pushes a normal contrast to an extreme. For example, making type "big" isn't enough. *Making type so big that the edges are indistinct* works because it forces an interaction of figure/ground. Here (immediately left) is an example that repeats parts of a single letter *c*.

Some typefaces are inherently abstract and hard to read. With these, ordinary typesetting is all that's needed to create an attention-getting abstracted message.

spabefgomty ɴʟᴀʙᴜᴇᴛᴏᴍᴇɴ Spabefgomty
ʃpabefgomty Spabefgomty CPABEFGOMTY

A typeface's character may be corroborative (**Nuclear**), opposing (Nuc|Ear), or neutral (Nuclear) to the meaning of its message. Use typography that is laden with character sparingly, only in the primary and secondary type where its attention-getting strength is at least as important as its legibility.

Typographic expression and playfulness is best done with relatively plain typefaces. Simple letterforms are editable while keeping their essential shapes legible. For this reason, sans serif faces are more useful than serif, and roman is more useful than italic.

**FRANKLIN CHAIR OCEAN SPACE
GOTHIC CRUMP SCREW STITCH
CONDENSED GRID SLASH TREE**

Tops of letters are easier to read than bottoms. Lowercase are easier to read than caps because word shapes are varied. Sometimes abstracting a word by leaving letters out entirely is the best way to get an idea across (near left).

Deaf college opens doors to hearing

Local school dropouts cut in half

by Karla Kohn

Deaf college opens doors to hearing

Local school dropouts cut in half

by Karla Kohn

Deaf college opens doors to hearing

Local school dropouts cut in half

by Karla Kohn

HAVÍRSKÁ · STARÉ MĚSTO · PRAHA 1

Killer sentenced to die for second time in ten years

Miners refuse to work after death

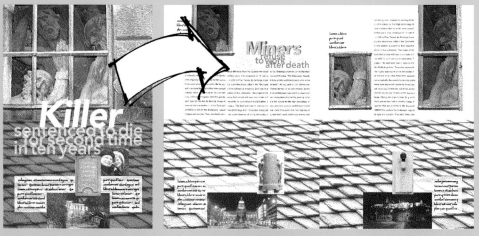

STOLEN PAINTING FOUND BY TREE

DRUNK GETS VIOLIN CASE

RED TAPE

HOLD UP

NEW BRIDGE

Story by Klaus Bürle
Photos by Milan Kincl

"Mala Strana couple slain"
Police suspect homicide

Secondary type

C **Subheads** are secondary type that explain headlines. A *deck* is a subhead immediately beneath the headline. A *floating subhead* is placed away from the headline. A *breaker head* is placed in the text column and, while breaking copy into short chunks, hints at the worthwhile goodies within.

If the headline is the lure, the subhead is the readers' payoff. Here is the opportunity to hook the reader by explaining the headline. The headline leads to one or more secondary messages, first a subhead or deck, but possibly a caption, breakout, or pull quote. The messages in the headline and subhead should be two parts of a complete thought, provocatively showing why the story is important to the reader. Readers should, after a total of three or four information "hits," have been given enough information about the story to make an informed decision about whether or not to get into the text. Actually becoming committed to the text can happen only after they have begun reading it.

C **Breakouts and pull quotes** are *brief* extracts from the text that are handled like verbal illustrations. Provocatively edited, their purpose is to make browsers stop and *consider* reading the story. Breakouts and pull quotes can visually connect pages of a long story by interpreting the type treatment of the opener's headline.

Secondary type should be smaller – or less visible – than the headline, but more prominent than text. A balance must be struck between contrasts and unity among the three levels of type. Variations of one typeface in the primary and secondary type contrast well against a highly legible text face.

Selecting the right typeface is a significant decision, but *how* you use a typeface is at least as important as *what* typeface is used. Imagine if your work were given an award for design excellence: would the typeface designer get the credit or would you be recognized for having used type well?

C **Captions** explain photos. Because they are read before the text, they must be thought of as display type and written short. Captions can unify a story by reinterpreting the headline. A caption can even be treated like a subhead or breakout.

A friend redesigned a magazine in the days of hot metal type, when a font was truly a single typeface in one size and weight. The foreign client had purchased only two fonts: 11-point Franklin Gothic Regular and Bold. The magazine could only use those two fonts, yet they had to do all that a magazine's typography must do. The redesign, using position and emptiness to make display type visible, succeeded because of – rather than in spite of – the extremely limited typographic contrast.

Avenir Black
Avenir Medium
Avenir Oblique
Loire Sombre
Loire Pale
Loire Pale Italique

Use no more than two typeface families in a design, and do not use more than two weights of each face (near left). Add italic versions of the regular weight and you have six typographic "voices," which should be enough to convey any message. This is equivalent to hearing six people reading aloud.

Seventy percent
Eighty percent
Ninety percent
One hundred percent
One hundred ten percent
e hundred twenty percent
e hundred thirty percent

Seventy percent
Eighty percent
Ninety percent
One hundred percent
e hundred ten percent
dred twenty percent
ndred thirty percent

-3 -4 0 -2 -3

Torskü   Torskü   Torskü

TRACKING "NORMAL"   TRACKING "TIGHT"   TRACKING "NORMAL"
NO KERNING   NO KERNING   *WITH KERNING*

☼ SMALL CAPS
TRUE SMALL CAPS ARE FOUND
IN SPECIAL "SC" FONTS

⛈ SMALL CAPS
FALSE SMALL CAPS ARE REDUCED
IN SIZE AND LOOK TOO LIGHT

☼ SMALL CAPS
TRUE SMALL CAPS ARE FOUND
IN SPECIAL "SC" FONTS

⛈ SMALL CAPS
FALSE SMALL CAPS ARE REDUCED
IN SIZE AND LOOK TOO LIGHT

Man minus ear waives
hearing

Man minus
ear waives
hearing

Man minus ear
waives hearing

Steals
clock,
faces
time

Steals
clock,
faces
time

STEALS
CLOCK,
FACES
TIME

STEALS
CLOCK,
FACES
TIME

℃ **Digitally compressing or expanding type** creates visual static at a certain point, which varies with each typeface. Shown here are a serif and a sans serif, both of which become visibly distorted at below 90 percent and above 110 percent of normal width.

℃ **Kerning** is the optical spacing of letterform pairs, which is more important than global tracking at display sizes.

℃ **Small caps** match the weight of full-size caps. False small caps,which are merely reduced in size, look too light because they are *proportionally* smaller.

"Quotation"

23' 9"

◑ **Real quote marks** look like "66" and "99." The inch (") and foot (') marks are incorrectly used as ambidextrous quote marks.

◔ **My top ten typefaces:**

Spagefomtie
Franklin Gothic

Spagefomti
Monotype Grotesque

Spagefomtie
Meta

Spagefomtie
News Gothic

Spagefomtie
Quay

Spagefomt
Clarendon

Spagefomtie
Loire

Spagefomtie
Menhart Manuscript

Spagefomtie
Nicolas Jenson SG

Spagefomtie
Californian

Setting display type

Display type shows off misspaced characters more than text simply because of its larger size, where character-to-character relationships are particularly visible. Letters are strung together into words. The space between individual letters goes unnoticed when the type is smaller than about 18 points. The optimum letterspacing is "invisible," that is, it is *un*-selfconscious. The reader should not be aware that letterspacing exists when it is done well.

Words are grouped into lines of type. Word spacing is the glue that holds lines of type together. The secret to good word spacing is also invisibility. The reader should not be aware of the type that is being read but should be concentrating on its meaning. Display word spacing is often too large because it is set with built-in text algorithms. In general, display type's global word spacing can be reduced to 50 to 80 percent of normal.

Headlines are made of clusters of phrases and should be "broken for sense" into these clusters, regardless of the shape this forces on the headline (facing page, fourth row). To find the natural breaks, read a headline out loud. Try not to break a headline to follow a design; rather, break a headline so that it *makes the most sense to the reader.* Hyphenating type communicates that shape is more important than meaning. Display type should never be hyphenated, unless its meaning is to illustrate "disconnection."

The effectiveness of display typography is principally dependent on the management of the white space between and around the letterforms, not only on the letterforms themselves. Because display type is brief (to snag the reader's attention), letterspacing, word spacing, and line breaks become more important.

Increase contrast and visibility of headlines by making them darker on the page. Reduce white space in and around characters in letterspacing and linespacing (facing page, bottom). All-cap headlines in particular should have linespacing removed because there are no descenders to "fill in" the space between lines. In upper- and lowercase settings, don't let ascenders and descenders touch, or they'll create an unintentional stigma on the page.

turkeyshavebeenbred

Orth
atBu
tter
ball
bird
sare
pick
edbe

caus
ethe
yloo
kgoo
dina
Butt
erba
llbag.

tohavewhitefeathersothebirdswillookappetizing

afterthey'vebeenplucked

Here we are now   at the middle
          of the fourth large part   of this talk.
More and more
nowhere.   Slowly   I have the feeling
                   we are getting   as the talk goes on
only irritating   It is not irritating   and that is a pleasure
                   to think one would like Here we are now
fourth large part a little bit after the middle   of the
                                           of this talk
          More and more   we have the feeling
          that I am getting   nowhere.
          Slowly
                                           as the talk goes on
slowly   we have the feeling
we are getting   That is a pleasure
which will continue   nowhere.   If we are irritated
          it is not a pleasure   Nothing is not   a
          if one is irritated   but suddenly
pleasure it is a pleasure   and then more and more
          it is not irritating   (and then more and more
and slowly   ).   Originally
          we were nowhere   and now, again
          slowly   the pleasure   If anybody
of being   nowhere.   let him go to sleep
is sleepy   W
Here we are now   at the beginning   of the
ninth unit of the fourth large part   as the talk goes on
More and more   we are getting
nowhere.   Slowly   and that is a pleasure
                   we are getting   It is
only irritating   It is not irritating   to be where one is   a
                   to think one would like little bit after the of
fourth large part a little bit after the beginning   of the ninth unit   of the
                                           of this talk
          More and more   we have the feeling

COLLAPSE

COLLAPSE FONT WAS DESIGNED IN 1993, ESPECIALLY
FOR A BROCHURE FOR THE ACADEMY OF FINE ARTS   AND
DESIGN IN BRATISLAVA, SLOVAKIA. IT IS A SINGLE   USE
TYPEFACE; I HAVE NOT USED IT SINCE THEN, AND PROBABLY
I WILL NEVER USE IT AGAIN. AS THE NAME OF THE   FONT
MAY SAY, COLLAPSE IS HIGHLY AFFECTED BY A NEW WAY OF
DESIGNING-COMPUTER GRAPHIC, AND BY THE COMPUTER
ERRORS THAT ARE CONNECTED WITH IT. THIS SEEMED TO BE
A SATISFACTORY REASON FOR ME TO DESIGN A NEW FONT.
BECAUSE OF A CHARACTER OF THE TASK (STUDENTS' EXHIBITION)
THE TYPEFACE WAS AIMED TO BE "NONTRADITIONAL".
ANOTHER REASON FOR THE CREATION OF THIS TYPEFACE
WAS THE LACK OF MONEY: WE COULD NOT AFFORD TO BUY   A
FONT, AND TO MAKE ONE UP AS A SCHOOL PROJECT DOES NOT COST
ANYTHING.

IN ORDER TO GIVE THE FACE A RANDOM LOOK, EVERY
LETTER HAS TWO DIFFERENT VERSIONS, SO THE FONT EXISTS
IN TWO DIFFERENT SETS-UPPER AND LOWER CASE.

UPPER CASE
LOWER CASE

タイラーの魅力が
十分に発揮された
秋冬コレクション

懐かしのブリティッシュ・アイテム

リ チャード・タイラーによ
るアンクラインのコレク
ションは、今シーズンでまだ2
回目だ。しかし彼は、故アン・ク
ライン女史の精神を損なうこと
なく、今の感覚をデザインに取
り込むことに成功、コレクショ
ンでは絶賛を浴びた。彼はニュ
ーヨークで最高のジャケットの
作り手と言われている。さまざま
なシルエット、素材。

もともとは男性のジャケットであった。ノーフォークジャケッ
ト共布のベルトが女性的になってからも、スポーティな活動着として活用。素材はヘリンボーン。
ジャケット¥89000/パンツ¥49000/
ジャケット¥29000/タキシード〈アンクライン〉
靴/アングローバル ショップ〈グレンソンブーツ〉

CÍNSKÝ PAVILLON

MIKOLÁŠ ALEŠ
1852
1913

13

C Textus to text (far left): Eric Gill, Buckinghamshire, 1931; Aldus Manutius, Venice, 1505; and St. John Hornby, London, 1902. **Weight, stress, and density** determine type's texture, as illustrated by this student exercise (near left).

C Type's space is imaginatively used in *Silence*, a collaboration by composer John Cage and typographer Raymond Grimaila (far left). **Variable character spacing** affects the text's right edge in this study by Peter Bil'ak (near left).

"The greatest literary masterpiece is no more than an alphabet in disorder." Jean Cocteau (1889–1963)

C Word spaces were nearly nonexistent in Nicolas Jenson's 1470 *Eusebius*. They had widened by 1761 in John Baskerville's *Aesop's Fables*. These samples (far left) are upside-down to show the spacing. **Japanese uses line spacing** to indicate horizontal or vertical reading. Note the additional typographic texture this provides (near left).

C Paragraph widths have been sized to align in this example (far left). **Text columns (near left)** nearly abut, but their baselines are staggered to indicate line ends.

*N*o matter how fine are the types we select, our work's appearance depends on good composition: the combination of type into words, the arrangement of words in lines, and the assemblage of lines to make pages. – D.B. Updike (1860–1941)

The term *text* comes from *textus*, Latin for the texture of woven fabric. There are two interpretations of this etymology, one that is conceptual and one that is visual: that text blends ideas and words into a single message as threads are woven into cloth; and that text areas have a visual texture that suggests fabric. Just as cloth's texture varies with the weight and material of the threads being used, type's texture depends on the letterforms' weight, angle of stress, and density.

Space and text type

■ **Between characters:** Remember, space between a pair of characters is *kerned*. Space between all characters in a paragraph is *tracked*. Optimal text character spacing must be more open than display type's to compesate for its small point size.

■ **Between words:** Word spacing is seen in proportion to letterspacing. If type has tight letterspacing, word spacing should be tight. Optimal word spacing is inconspicuous and barely separates word-thoughts without breaking the line into chunks.

■ **Between lines:** Optimal line spacing must be greater than word spacing, so the eye travels horizontally; the space should be sufficient so descenders and ascenders don't overlap, but not so great that it breaks up the integrity of the column.

■ **Between paragraphs:** A paragraph contains a single idea. Each idea must be perceived both as an entity and as part of a string of ideas. Separate paragraphs with an indent, a hanging indent, or

with additional space between paragraphs. ⁊ Paragraphing may also be achieved through use of a dingbat, allowing continuous text. The first paragraph of text should never be indented: it spoils the clean left corner and it is a duplicate signal because the typographic contrast between deck and text has already indicated the beginning of a new idea.

■ **Between text columns:** Optimal column spacing must be greater than a word space so that readers won't accidently jump the gutter while reading, but not so great that the columns look unrelated. A pica space between columns and between text and image in a runaround is optimal to separate but not dissociate.

Text abstraction

While it is good to abstract display type, text type should be treated so its legibility is paramount. Energy has been spent designing the imagery and display type to lure the browser into the text, where the greatest story value can be found. After successfully getting the reader into the text, yours has been a wasted effort if the reader bails out because the text has too many characters per line, or is poorly spaced, or too small, or too light, or a busy background makes reading impossible.

This isn't to say you can't reveal meaning in the way text is handled. When text abstraction is to the point, readers *may* respond. "A free-shaped area, wherever it occurs, must be a spontaneous and natural typographic expression of the copy; the copy should almost insist, of its own accord, that it be set this way," wrote Carl Dair in *Design with Type*. Similarly, Bradbury Thompson believes, "A sense of freedom to forget the columns and grids of typographic traditions lets the designer work in an atmosphere in which to playfully mix words and images."

Abstracting text to make a point is a worthy aim, but caution is key: abstraction is dangerous because text's small size makes illegibility a constant worry. And besides, using abstraction in text to catch an already caught reader is a waste of energy.

Acegmorty spabefgomty wundrick vox dahlz whim quest ace mordich al safen gomby spago *Centaur Regular 12pt*

Acegmorty spabefgomty wun drick vox dahlz whim quest ace mordich al safen gomby *Menhart Manuscript Regular 10pt*

Acegmorty spabefgomty wun drick vox dahlz whim quest ace mordich al safen gomby spago famenice *Ellington Regular 9pt*

Acegmorty spabefgomty wun drick vox dahlz whim quest ace mordich al safe gomty spagofa *Futura No.2 12pt*

Acegmorty spabefgomty wun drick vox dahlz whim quest ace mordich al safe gomty spa *Bell Gothic Roman 10.5pt*

Acegmorty spabefgomty wun drick vox dahlz whim quest ace mordich al safe gomby spagofa *Interstate Light 9pt*

Serif type can be set with no additional linespacing because its serifs force open letterspacing and emphasize horizontality. This is 10/10 Nicolas Jenson SG set across a 9-pica column. There are and average of about 30 characters per line. Serif type can be set with no addi-

Sans serif type lacks the serifs that aid reading. This paragraph is set as if it were serif type: no additional linespacing and no letterspacing adjustment. This is 10/10 News Gothic Regular set across a 9-pica column, with an average of 32 characters per line. Sans serif type lacks the

This is an improved sans serif paragraph, set with 2 points of additional linespacing and 10 percent increased letter-spacing. It is 10/12 News Gothic set across a 9-pica column, with an average of 28.5 characters per line. This is

This paragraph is set 10/12 with too many characters per line for optimal legibility. Well-set text has 50 to 60 characters per line, including spaces and punctuation. This paragraph has about 80 characters per line, or 25 characters more than it should, making this text tiring to read for more than two or, at most, three lines. To maximize legibility, there must be more linespacing, enough to make a white bar for each return.

There are two ways to get 50-60 characters per line. One is to enlarge the type and keep the measure. The other is to

keep the type size and the line spacing, but shorten the measure to the correct length of fifty to sixty characters per line. This paragraph is set 10/12 with an average of 58 characters per line for optimal legibility. This para-

A flush-left setting puts all excess space at the right end of each line. Word spaces are all exactly the same width and make reading easier. There are two kinds of ragged edge,

A justified setting divides excess space between word spaces and characters. This looks bad when there is too much space and too few spaces. A justified setting divides

Properly set justified text requires a minimum of five word spaces per line to absorb leftover space. This makes the variations among word spaces less conspicuous. Properly set justified text requires a minimum of five word spaces per line to absorb leftover space. This makes the variations among word spaces

⌐ Text type should be sized according to its x-height, the height of the lowercase letter from baseline to median. The x-height, not the overall point size, is the dimension that makes type appear "small" or "big."

⌐ Serif versus sans serif: Serif can be easier to read at text sizes because serifs create open letterspacing and strong horizontality. Serif faces also have more contrast between thick and thin strokes. Compensate by adding line- and letterspacing to sans serif settings.

⌐ Line length should be 50–60 characters per line for maximum legibility. Lines with more than 60 characters require additional linespacing so readers can easily trace back to the left edge of the column. A typeface with a large x-height requires more linespacing than a face with a small x-height, which has "built-in" horizontal space.

⌐ Justified versus flush left: A justified setting distributes extra space on each line, but there must be at least five word spaces to disguise the variations. Flush left is easier to set well. The only decisions are whether to allow hyphenation (always), and where to set the hyphenation zone (half a pica is best).

Effortless text

Text type must be effortless to read, that is, it must be without visual static. This is achieved by choosing a good typeface, making it big enough to read, giving it invisible letter, word, and linespacing, and giving it maximum contrast with its background. This paragraph has all the attributes that should not be given to text: it is bold italic, which can only be read in very short passages; it is small, 9-point type, which cannot be followed for more than forty characters per line; the letter and word spacing has been tightened to 60 percent of normal; the linespacing has been set solid, meaning the necessary horizontal white bars between lines of type have been reduced to uselessness; and the contrast between type and its background has been compromised by an illustration. Why would I make this text so hard for you to read? Maybe I am unaware of the difficulty I am causing. Maybe I think it would entertain you to have a whale in the background. Or maybe I think it would be novel to try these "stylings" because I am bored setting type so it is "ordinary" and legible.

Some text types are inherently more legible and should be chosen over other faces. A legible face should then be sized for clarity. Text ranges from 9 to 12 points, but faces with large x-heights can be set from 9 to 11 points, while faces with small x-heights should be set from 10 to 12 points for visual equivalency.

Consistent spacing is crucial to making text attractive and easy to read. Poor type comes from letting the computer's default settings determine spacing attributes. Text should always be defined as a "style," so every attribute will be considered in its definition. The goal for well-set text is a smooth, even color.

Justifying text is a process that results in a smooth right edge, as in this paragraph of text. The extra space at the end of each line is equally divided among the word spaces on that line. When there aren't enough words per line, this creates exaggerated word spaces. When a few such lines with poor spacing are stacked, they form a "river" of white, an ugly vertical line (see page 114).

Flush-left text has consistent word and character spacing because all leftover space is in a chunk at the end of the line. The resulting right column edge is said to be "ragged." A "rough rag" is produced by turning off hyphenation. A "tight rag," in which the lines are more even, is made by setting the hyphenation zone to a half-pica or less.

Text type often has its own latent shape and structure. For example, a recipe is entirely different copy from an interview. Setting a recipe as if it were dialogue would not express its step-by-step nature. Recognizing the nature of the copy at hand leads to the right decisions that will produce authentic typography.

Setting perfect text

OUR USE OF TYPE is based on centuries of typographic evolution, hundreds of improvements based on efficiency and economy in our need to record and distribute ideas. Perfect typography is a logical art. It is based on harmony in all its parts. The right decisions are those that get the message to the reader with the least visual static.

As Ms. C. L. Janáková said in 1915, "The spaces after periods in names should be half the width" of a normal word space. Never leave two spaces after a period. "Alot" is *always* two words, "a lot."

It sometimes seems there are fifty tiny typographic steps to setting perfect text.

Setting perfect text

OUR USE OF TYPE is based on centuries of typographic evolution, hundreds of improvements based on efficiency and economy in our need to record and distribute ideas.

Perfect typography is a *logical* art. It is based on harmony in all its parts. The right decisions are those that get the message to the reader with the least visual static.

As Ms. C. L. Jánaková said in 1915, "The space after periods in a name should be half the width" of a normal word space. Never leave two spaces after a period. "Alot" is *always* two words, "a lot."

It sometimes seems there are fifty tiny typographic steps to setting perfect text.

Setting perfect text

Informed use of type compensates for the "incorrect" application of typographic conventions. Shown here are the most important adjustments for day-to-day use.

To ignore or neglect these adjustments is to allow your type to be mere data entry. Attending to these details distinguishes work as being valuable and worthy of the reader's time and as having been done by an informed designer, which makes you look good.

The computer standardizes and repeats very well. Use its strength by creating paragraph styles. This forces you to choose, which leads to *conscious* spacing attributes. It also makes document–wide changes easy: a change in the style definition changes all type tagged with that definition. Text type in discreet blocks, each with its own *ad hoc* style, leads to inconsistencies.

Hyphenate all text yourself, whether set in justified or flush-left lines. Built-in hyphenation dictionaries invariably fail: keep a paperback 50,000 word speller at hand and use it.

Indentions, in points to match the linespacing (type's point size plus leading), should be part of the paragraph's style definition.

A widow is a short phrase, word, or part of a word that is a paragraph's last line. An orphan is a widow at the top of a column. Widows are generally okay, but orphans will get you a reprimand from the Type Police. Absorb a widow by manually forcing tighter spacing on the next-to-last line by selecting it and pressing Option-Delete (Mac) or Shift-Control-minus (PC).

Fractions like ¼, ½, and ¾ can be found in expert fonts. Any fraction can be made from three pieces: the numerator (top number) is set in superscript (in *Define Styles*, set *Super/subscript size* at 60 percent, and *Superscript position* at 28 percent) and the denominator (bottom number) is set in subscript (in *Define Styles*, set *Subscript position* at 0 percent).

Perfect text is one element of a successful page. But the success of a page is only as good as the power with which it communicates and the effortlessness with which it does it.

Side notes

🎧 **Indent turnovers on bulleted lists** to make beginnings clear. Set a style with a 1p0 left indent; -1p0 first line; and a tab at 1p0.

🎧 **Align decimals in charts** to make figures comparable. Use the ↓˙ arrow on the tab ruler.

🎧 **An ellipsis** is a three-dot character that indicates a pause or an extracted segment. It is *not* the same as three periods.

"In the end, writing that is read must be *intended* to be read.... There is an implicit obligation for the designer to mediate between text and reader."
William Drenttel

Glossary

Aldine Typography that appears to have come from Venitian printer Aldus Manutius, c1500.

Alignment Having elements' edge placement agree. Optical alignment is always more important than measurable alignment.

Aperture See *Counter.*

Apex The area of a letterform where two lines meet as in A, M, V, W.

Archival paper Paper that is alkaline and won't deteriorate over time. Cannot contain any groundwood or unbleached wood fiber.

Ascender The part of lowercase letters that extend above the median in b, d, f, h, k, l, t. See *Descender.*

Backslant Type posture that slants to the left. Compare to *Italic,* which slants to the right. Uncommon and difficult to read in any but extremely short segments.

Bar The horizontal stroke of a letterform like F, H, T, Z.

Baseline Invisible line on which letterforms sit.

Basic size A sheet size for each of the standard paper grades that determines its basis weight. The basic size of book paper is 25"x 38". The basic size of cover stock is 20"x 26".

Basis weight The weight in pounds of a ream (500 sheets) of paper cut to its basic size.

Beardline Invisible line that indicates the bottom of descenders.

Binding Attaching sheets of paper together for ease of use and protection. There are four methods of binding: edition binding, 16-page signatures stitched together; mechanical binding, plastic rings or combs inserted in drilled holes; perfect binding, whereby glue is spread on the pages' edges and a cover is applied; saddle-stitched binding, stapled through the fold; and side-stitched binding, stapled through the front.

Bitmap A character image represented as a pattern of dots on a screen. See *Outline.*

Blackletter Heavy, angular types based on medieval script writing. The five categories of blackletter are Bastarda, Fraktur, Quadrata, Rotunda, and Textura.

Bleed Imagery or letterforms that run off the trimmed edge of a page. See *Full bleed.*

Blind folio A page that has no visible page number printed on it. In magazines, often found on feature openers with full bleed imagery.

Body copy The primary text of a story. Usually identified by a medium weight and a body size of 8 to 12 points.

Body size See *Point size.*

Bold A typeface style that is heavier and wider than the roman style of the same typeface.

Brightness The reflectivity of paper. Lower brightness absorbs more light, making reading more difficult. Higher brightness means a whiter sheet of paper, costs more, and lends a sense of quality.

Cap height The height of capital letters, measured from baseline to top of the letterforms.

Centered Alignment in which the midpoints of each element are positioned on a central axis. The left and right edges of such a column are mirror images.

Chancery A handwritten typestyle with long, graceful ascenders and descenders.

Character Any letter, numeral, punctuation mark, figure, etc.

Character set The letters, figures, punctuation marks, and symbols that can be displayed on a monitor or output by a printer.

Coated paper Paper with a layer of matte, dull, or gloss coating applied. Coated paper keeps ink from absorbing into the paper, making images crisp and bright.

Cold type Printing which is not produced by the hot-metal process. Involves the use of founders' type, phototypesetting, or electronic (digital) setting. See *hot metal.*

Colophon Information placed at the end of a book that describes its production.

Color, typographic The lightness or darkness of gray that a type area creates. Typographic color is affected by the type's size, posture, weight, linespacing, and tracking.

Column rule A thin line between columns of type.

Condensed A narrow version of a typeface.

Contrast The degree of difference between light and dark areas in an image. Extreme lights and darks are high contrast. A full range of grays is low contrast.

Contrast, typographic The amount of variation between thick and thin strokes of a letter.

Counter The space, either completely or only partially closed, in letterforms like a, e, o, u, and A, B, C, S.

Crop marks Thin lines added to the perimeter of a design to show where to trim the finished print job.

Cursive Typefaces with fluid strokes that look like handwriting.

Deinking Removing ink and other additives from paper in the recycling process.

Descender The part of lowercase letters that extend below the baseline in g, j, p, q, y. See *Ascender*.

Dingbat Illustrative characters in a typeface.

Display type Letterforms whose purpose is to be read first. Usually identified by a large body size and bold weight.

dpi Abbreviation for dots per inch, a measure of resolution.

Drop cap A large initial set into the top left corner of body copy. A drop cap's baseline must align with a text baseline. See *Stickup initial*.

Drop folio A page number placed at the bottom of a page when most page numbers are positioned at the tops of pages, as in the first page of a chapter of a novel.

Dummy An unprinted mock-up of a book, magazine, or brochure.

Duotone A two-color halftone, usually black and a second ink color. The result is an image with more richness and depth than a one-color halftone.

Ear Small stroke attached to the *g* and *r*.

Ellipsis A single character of three dots indicating an ommission. The spacing of an ellipsis (...) is generally distinct from three periods in a row (...).

Em dash The longest dash in a typeface. An em dash is the same width as the type size being used: 10-point type, which is measured vertically, has a 10-point-wide em dash. The em dash separates thoughts within a sentence and should not have spaces added on either side: xxxx—xxxx. I frequently bend this rule, replacing the em dash with an en dash surrounded by two spaces: xxxx – xxxx; the em dash is simply too wide in many typefaces and draws attention to itself.

En dash The second-longest dash in a typeface. An en dash is half the width of the type size being used: 10-point type, measured vertically, has a 5-point wide en-dash. The en dash separates numbers and should not have spaces added on either side: 555–666. Also used in place of a hyphen for multiple-compound words.

Extended A wider version of a typeface. Also called *expanded*.

Ethel A French ligature of the *o* and *e* letters, found in Greek words.

Family A group of typefaces derived from the same typeface design. Usually includes roman, italic, and bold versions. May include small caps, old style figures, expanded, condensed, and inline versions.

Finish The surface characteristics of paper.

Flush A typographic term meaning *aligned* or *even*. Type can be set flush left, even on the left and ragged on the right; flush right, even on the right and ragged on the left; or flush left and right, more properly called *justified*.

Folio A page number and running head.

Font A set of characters that share common characteristics. Also called *Typeface*.

Foot margin The space at the bottom of a page. See *Margin* and *Head margin*.

Foundry The place where type is manufactured. A foundry was originally a place for metalwork; modern typefoundries are digital.

Four-color process A printing process that uses magenta (red), cyan (blue), yellow, and black inks to simulate the continuous tones and variety of colors in a color image.

Full bleed Imagery or letterforms that run off all four edges of a page. See *Bleed*.

Gatefold A page that is folded inward to make an extended spread. The most famous gatefold is the *Playboy* centerfold.

Grain The direction that most fibers lie in a sheet of paper. This is important in folding and tearing.

Grotesque Another name for sans serif type. So called because it was considered ugly when it was introduced in the mid-1800s.

Gutter The space between columns of type and between facing pages of a book or magazine.

Hairline The thinnest line which an output device can make. Usually ¼ point.

Halftone A printed image in which continuous tone is reproduced as dots of varying sizes.

Hanging indent A paragraphing style in which the first line pokes out to the left. Sometimes called an *outdent* or *flush and hung*.

Hanging initial An initial letter placed in the margin next to body copy.

Hanging punctuation Allowing lines that begin or end with punctuation to extend a bit beyond the column width for optical alignment. A certain indicator of typographic sensitivity and craftsmanship.

Head margin The space at the top of a page. See *Margin* and *Foot margin*.

Hinting Mathematical formulas applied to outline fonts to improve the quality of their screen display and printing on low-resolution printers.

Hot metal Typesetting and the printing process that involves casting type from molten lead.

Humanist Letterforms that look a bit like handwriting, or at least don't look too mechanical or geometric. Identifiable by having a humanist axis, or angled emphasis related to handwriting.

Imposition Arranging pages so that when they are printed and trimmed, they will appear in correct order.

Incunabula "Cradle", used to describe the first fifty years of printing with moveable type.

Ink holdout Resistance to the penetration of ink. Coated paper has high ink holdout, making images look sharp.

Italic Types that slant to the right. Must have letters that are distinctly different from roman version of the typeface, like *a* and a, or it is probably an *oblique* version.

Justification Aligning both the left and right sides of a column of type.

Kern Removing space between specific letter pairs in order to achieve optically consistent letterspacing. See *Tracking*.

Leaders A line of dots that lead the eye across a wide space. Often found on contents listings.

Leading Space between lines of type that appears between the descenders of one line and the ascenders of the next. Digital leading is added *above* a given line of type. The name comes from hot metal days when actual strips of lead were inserted between lines of poured type.

Lead-in The first few words of a paragraph set to attract attention.

Legibility The ability to distinguish between letterforms. See *Readability*.

Letterspacing A term used to describe general spacing between letterforms. See *Kern* and *Tracking*.

Ligature Conjoined pairs or trios of characters into one, as in fi and ffl, for optical consistency.

Light or lightface A lighter variation of the density of a typeface.

Line spacing See *Leading*.

Lining figures Numerals that are equivalent to the cap height of the typeface. To be used in charts and in all-caps settings. Also called *ranging figures*. See *Old style figures*.

Margin The space at the inside and outside of a page. Also called *side margin*. See *Foot margin* and *Head margin*.

Match color A custom-blended ink that matches a specified color exactly. There are several systems, including Pantone Matching System and Toyo.

Median The invisible line that defines the top of lowercase letters that have no ascender. Also called *mean line* and *waist line*.

Minus leading Removing space between lines of type to give it a more unified and darker look. Should always be used with all caps display type and with great care on U/lc display type to keep ascenders and descenders from overlapping. See *Leading*.

Moiré A pattern created by rescreening a halftone. or by printing two halftones on top of each other but out of register. Pronounced *mwah-RAY*.

Monospace Typefaces in which each character occupies the same horizontal space. A leftover from typewriter technology. See *Variable space*.

NFNT Abbreviation for Macintosh font numbering system which assigns numbers to screen fonts.

Oblique An angled version of a roman typeface in which the same characters have been slanted to the right, not redrawn. See *Italic*.

Octothorp The number or pound sign (#). So named because it indicates eight farms surrounding a town square.

Old style figures Numerals that vary in height so they blend into a paragraph of text. Sometimes mistakenly called "lowercase figures." See *Lining figures*.

Opacity A measure of how opaque a sheet of paper is. Low opacity allows printing on the back side to show through. Opacity may be achieved through increasing sheet thickness or by adding chemical opacifiers.

Optical alignment Adjusting elements or letterforms so they appear aligned, which is more important than actually being aligned.

Orphan A word or word fragment at the top of a column. A sign of ultimate carelessness. See *Widow*.

Outline The mathematical representation of a character that can be scaled to any size and resolution.

Papyrus An aquatic plant found in northern Africa. Used as early writing substrate, it was peeled and placed in layers. The naturally-occuring glues in the fibers bonded into sturdy sheets.

Parchment A writing substrate made from treated animal skins.

Phototypesetting Setting type by means of light being exposed through a film negative of characters onto light-sensitive paper. Introduced in the 1960s and replaced by digital typesetting in the 1980s.

Pica One-sixth of an inch, or 12 points. Because it is divisible by points, and thus accommodates type measurement, it is necessary to use the pica for all planning design space. See *Point*.

Point One-seventy-second of an inch, or one-twelfth of a pica. The basic unit of vertical measurement of type. See *Pica*.

Point size The size of a typeface measured from just above the top of the ascenders to just beneath the bottom of the descenders. Also called *body size* and *type size*.

Posture The angle of stress of a typeface. There are three postures: roman, italic or oblique, and backslant.

Readability The quality of reading, determined by letterspacing, linespacing, paper-and-ink contrast, among other factors. See *Legibility*.

Recto The right-hand page of a spread. Always odd-numbered. See *Verso*.

Resolution The number of dots per inch (dpi) displayed on a screen or by a printer, which determines how smooth the curves and angles of characters appear. Higher resolution yields smoother characters.

Reversed out White or light color dropped out of a dark background.

Roman An upright, medium-weight typeface style.

Rough rag Type set without hyphenation, causing a pronounced variation in line length. See *Tight rag*.

Rule A line.

Runaround Type set around an image or element. The ideal distance is 1 pica, or enough space to separate, but not enough to dissociate the type and image from each other.

Sans serif Type without cross strokes at the ends of their limbs. Usually have consistent stroke weight.

Serif Type whose limbs end in cross strokes. Usually have variation in main character stroke weight.

Slab serif Type with especially thick serifs. All Egyptian typefaces are slab serifs.

Small caps Capital letters that are about the size of lowercase letters of the same typeface. Unlike using capital letters set a few points smaller, true small caps must be drawn to appear the same weight as their full-size capitals.

Solid Type set without additional linespacing.

Stickup initial A large initial set at the top left corner of body copy. A stickup initial's baseline must align with the first text baseline. Also called *elevated cap*. See *Drop cap*.

Style Variations of a typeface, including roman, italic, bold, condensed, and extended.

Subhead Secondary type that explains the headline and leads to the text.

Texture The overall impression of an area of type. Determined by typeface, size, linespacing, color, and column structure.

Tight rag Type set with a small hyphenation zone, causing minimal variation in line length. See *Rough rag*.

Tracking Adjusting space in a line or paragraph. See *Kern*.

Turnovers Type that continues on a subsequent line.

Typeface A set of characters of a certain design and bearing its own name, like Ephesus Ancient, Franklin Gothic, or Preissig.

Type family All styles and variations of a single typeface. May include italic, bold, small caps, etc.

Typographer Historically, one who sets type. In modern usage, one who practices the craft and art of designing letterforms and designing with letterforms.

Typography The art and craft of designing with type.

Type size See *Point size*.

U/lc Type setting using upper and lowercase letters.

Uncoated paper Paper without a surface coating.

Variable space Type in which each character is assigned its own width as determined by the characters' inherent widths. See *Monospace*.

Verso The left hand page of a spread. Always even-numbered. See *Recto*.

Watermark A mark in fine papers, embedded in the papermaking process with a dandy roll.

Weight The darkness of a typeface.

Widow A word or word fragment at the end of a paragraph. Words are okay, but word fragments are careless. See *Orphan*.

Word space Space between words. Sensitive to letterspacing: if one is open, both must be open. "Correct" word spacing is invisible: just enough to separate words but not enough to break a line of type into chunks. The lowercase *i* can be used as a guide for approximate spacing.

X-height The distance from the baseline to the median in lowercase letters. So named because it is the height of a lowercase *x*, which has neither an ascender nor a descender.

Bibliography

I have selected the most important books on design and typography in the last fifty years. Some I have only seen; many I own and love.

The important thing about a bibliography is to have a road sign that points to further knowledge on a subject. Discovering books that help you understand and see a vast subject like design and visual communication in a new way is worth the effort.

You may note that the majority of these books are released by the same few publishers. Visiting these publishers' Web sites will lead you to many other worthwhile texts.

Some of these books are out of print. Of these, a few are being made available again every year. Many can be found as out of print selections at on-line auction sites.

Aldis, Harry G. *The Printed Book.* New York: Cambridge University Press, 1951.

The Type Directors Club Annual. New York: HarperCollins Publishers, published annually.

Bartram, Alan. *Five Hundred Years of Book Design.* New Haven: Yale University Press, 2001.

Baudin, Fernand. *How Typography Works (and Why It Is Important).* New York: Design Press, 1988.

Berry, W. Turner, A.F. Johnson, and W.P. Jaspert. *An Encyclopedia of Typefaces.* London: Blandford Press, 1970.

Blackwell, Lewis. *20th Century Type (remix).* Corte Madera Calif.: Gingko Press Inc., 1998.

Bringhurst, Robert. *The Elements of Typographic Style.* Point Roberts, Wash.: Hartley & Marks, 1997. 2nd ed.

Budliger, Hansjörg. *Jan Tschichold: Typograph und Schriftentwerfer.* Zürich: Kunstgewerbemuseum, 1976.

Burns, Aaron. *Typography.* New York: Reinhold Publishing Corp., 1961.

Carter, Harry. *A View of Early Typography Up to About 1600.* Oxford: Clarendon Press, 1968.

Carter, Sebastian. *Twentieth Century Type Designers.* New York: W.W. Norton, 1995.

Chappell, Warren. *A Short History of the Printed Word.* Boston: David R. Godine, 1980.

Dair, Carl. *Design With Type.* 1952. Reprint, Toronto: University of Toronto Press, 1982.

Dormer, Peter. *Design Since 1945.* London: Thames & Hudson Ltd, 1993.

Dowding, Geoffrey. *Finer Points in the Spacing and Arrangement of Type.* 1957. Reprint, Point Roberts, Wash.: Hartley & Marks, 1995.

Dürer, Albrecht. *Of the Just Shaping of Letters.* New York: Dover, 1965.

Fertel, Dominique. *La Science Practique de l'Imprimerie.* 1723. Reprint: Farnborough, England: Gregg International, 1971.

Firmage, Richard A. *Alphabet Abecedarium: Some Note on Letters.* London: Bloomsbury Publishing, 2001.

Frutiger, Adrian. *Type Sign Symbol.* Zurich: ABC Edition, 1980.

Gill, Eric. *An Essay on Typography.* Boston: David R. Godine, 1988.

Ginger, E.M., S. Rögener, A-J. Pool, and U. Packhäuser. *Branding with Type: How Type Sells.* Mountain View, Calif.: Adobe Press, 1995.

Goudy, Frederic. *The Alphabet and Elements of Lettering.* Berkeley & Los Angeles: The University of California Press, 1942.

Heller, Steven, and Philip B. Meggs, eds. *Texts on Type: Critical Writings on Typography.* New York: Allworth Press, 2001.

Hlavsa, Oldrich. *A Book of Type and Design.* New York: Tudor Publishing, 1960.

Holland, DK. *Design Issues: How Graphic Design Informs Society.* New York: Allworth Press, 2001.

Hollis, Richard. *Graphic Design: A Concise History.* New York: Thames and Hudson, 1994.

Hutchinson, James. *Letters.* New York: Van Nostrand Reinhold Company, 1983.

Jean, Georges. *Writing: The Story of Alphabets and Scripts.* New York: Harry N. Abrams Inc., 1992.

Kelly, Rob Roy. *American Wood Type: 1828-1900, Notes on the Evolution of Decorated and Large Types.* New York: Da Capo, 1977.

Kohl, Herbert. *From Archetype to Zeitgeist: Powerful Ideas for Powerful Thinking.* Boston: Back Bay Books, 1992.

Lawson, Alexander. *Anatomy of a Typeface.* Boston: David R. Godine, 1990.

Loewy, Raymond. *Industrial Design.* Woodstock, N.Y.: The Overlook Press, 1979.

Lupton, Ellen. *Mixing Messages: Graphic Design in Contemporary Culture.* New York: Princeton Architectural Press, 1996.

Lupton, Ellen, and J. Abbott Miller. *Design Writing Research.* New York: Kiosk Books, 1996.

McCloud, Scott. *Understanding Comics: The Invisible Art.* New York: HarperCollins, 1994.

McLean, Rauri. *The Thames and Hudson Manual of Typography.* London & New York: Thames and Hudson, 1980.

McLean, Rauri. *Typographers on Type.* New York & London: W.W. Norton & Company, 1995.

Merriman, Frank. *A.T.A. Type Comparison Book.* Advertising Typographers Association of America, 1965.

Miller, J. Abbott. *Dimensional Typography.* New York: Princeton Architectural Press, 1996.

Morison, Stanley. *A Tally of Types.* Jaffrey, N.H.: David R. Godine Publisher, Inc., 1999.

Morison, Stanley. *First Principles of Typography.* Cambridge University Press, 1967. *2nd Ed.*

Morison, Stanley. *On Type Designs Past and Present: A Brief Introduction.* London: Ernest Benn, 1962.

Morison, Stanley, and Kenneth Day. *The Typographic Book 1450-1935; A Study of Fine Typography Through Five Centuries.* Chicago: The University of Chicago Press, 1963.

Müller-Brockmann, Joseph. *Grid Systems in Graphic Design: A Visual Communication Manual for Graphic Designers, Typographers and Three Dimensional Designers.* New York: Visual Communication Books, Hastings House Publishers, 1981.

Negroponte, Nicholas. *Being Digital.* New York: Basic Books, 1995.

Norton, Robert. *Types Best Remembered, Types Best Forgotten.* Kirkland, Wash.: Parsimony Press, 1993.

Ogg, Oscar. *Arrighi, Tagliente, Palatino - Three Classics of Italian Calligraphy.* New York: Dover Publications, 1953.

Owen, William. *Modern Magazine Design.* Dubuque, Iowa: Wm. C. Brown Publishers, 1992.

Pederson, B. Martin. *Graphis Book Design I.* Zurich: Graphis Press Corp., 1995.

Pederson, B. Martin. *Graphis Typography I.* Zurich: Graphis Press Corp., 1994.

Rand, Paul. *A Designer's Art.* New Haven: Yale University Press, 1985.

Reed, Talbot B. *A History of the Old English Letter Foundries.* London: Faber and Faber Ltd., 1952.

Remington, R. Roger, and Barbara J. Hodik. *Nine Pioneers in American Graphic Design.* Cambridge, Mass.: The MIT Press, 1989.

Rogers, Bruce. *Paragraphs on Printing.* New York: Dover Publications, 1979.

Romano, Frank J. *The TypEncyclopedia.* New York and London: R.R. Bowker Company, 1984.

Rondthaler, Edward. *Life with Letters...As They Turned Photogenic.* New York: Visual Communication Books, Hastings House Publishers, 1981.

Rothschild, Deborah, Ellen Lupton, and Darra Goldstein. *Graphic Design in the Mechanical Age.* New Haven: Yale University Press, 1998.

Ruder, Emil. *Typography: A Manual of Design.* Adapted by Charles Bigelow. New York: Hastings House, 1981.

Spencer, Herbert, ed. *The Liberated Page.* San Francisco: Bedford Press, 1987.

Spencer, Herbert. *Pioneers of Modern Typography.* Cambridge, Massachusetts: The MIT Press, 1982. *2nd ed.*

Spiekermann, Erik. *Rhyme & Reason: A Typographic Novel.* Berlin: H. Berthold AG, 1987.

Spiekermann, Erik, and E.M. Ginger. *Stop Stealing Sheep and Find Out How Type Works.* Mountain View, Calif.: Adobe Press, 1993.

Steinberg, S.H. *Five Hundred Years of Printing.* Harmondsworth, England: Penguin Books, 1974.

Thompson, Bradbury. *The Art of Graphic Design.* New Haven: Yale University Press, 1988.

Tracy, Walter. *Letters of Credit: A View of Type Design.* Boston: David R. Godine, 1989.

Tschichold, Jan. *Asymmetric Typography.* Trans. by Rauri McLean. London: Faber and Faber, 1967.

Tschichold, Jan. *The New Typography.* 1928. Trans. by Rauri McLean. Berkeley: University of California Press, 1995.

Tschichold, Jan. *The Form of the Book: Essays on the Morality of Good Design.* Trans. by Hajo Hadeler. Point Roberts, Wash.: Hartley & Marks, 1991.

White, Alex W. *Type in Use, Second Ed.* New York: W.W. Norton, 1999.

White, Jan V. *Editing by Design; Graphic Design for the Electronic Age; Graphic Idea Notebook.* Rowayton, Connecticut: The Helix Press, 2001.

White, Jan V. *Great Pages.* El Segundo: Serif Publishing, 1990.

Williamson, Hugh. *Methods of Book Design.* New Haven: Yale University Press, 1983.

Wilson, Adrian. *The Design of Books.* San Francisco: Chronicle Books, 1993.

Designer's checklist

Questions that should be answered with a "yes" ⊡ **are in bold.** Questions that should be answered with a "no" ☐ are in regular weight.

Space

- ⊡ **Do all areas of white space look like they were planned and thoughtfully used?**
- ⊡ **Is the ground as interesting as the figures on it?**
- ⊡ **Is space between elements strictly controlled and consistent?**
- ⊡ **Is space used to signal quality and value?**
- ⊡ **Is there a payoff for having this emptiness?**
- ⊡ **Does empty space define an object's relative size?**
- ⊡ **Are related topics close and unrelated ones separated?**
- ⊡ **Can the background be brought into the foreground?**
- ⊡ **Can overfullness (*lack* of emptiness) be used to describe this content?**
- ⊡ **Is empty space activated for contrast and visibility rather than merely left over?**
- ⊡ **Has space been removed from headlines to make them darker and more visible?**
- ⊡ **Is empty space used to make an opening page or spread look nonthreatening and inviting?**
- ⊡ **Are areas of white space balanced with occupied space?**
- ⊡ **Can emptiness be used representationally or symbolically?**
- ⊡ **Has the especially visible emptiness around the perimeter of the page been used?**
- ⊡ **Is space used to emphasize either horizontality or verticality?**
- ☐ Have consistent, systematic spaces between elements been compromised to fill a short column?
- ☐ Can space be better managed in and around typographic elements?
- ☐ Does any element appear to be floating separately on the page?
- ☐ Does the page look crowded?
- ☐ Could the empty areas be called "wasted space"?
- ☐ Is emptiness just in the background?
- ☐ Are mere boxes and rules – rather than differences expressed through position, size, and weight – used to organize space?

Unity

- ⊡ **Are all elements cooperating to make a single impression?**
- ⊡ **Are contrasts clear enough to look purposeful?**
- ⊡ **Is there a dominant element that will transfix the casual browser?**
- ⊡ **Are elements sized in proportion to their importance?**
- ⊡ **Has design unity been enhanced by limiting type and color pallettes?**
- ⊡ **Does color emphasize what is worthy of emphasis?**
- ⊡ **Is color used to explain content rather than decorate the page?**
- ⊡ **Is the stopping power of huge images used?**
- ⊡ **Is there a cheerful variety or is the total effect gray and pallid?**
- ⊡ **Have similar elements been grouped?**
- ⊡ **Are relationships between elements immediately apparent?**
- ⊡ **Do the shapes of elements add contrast and visual interest?**
- ⊡ **Do art elements accurately and distinctively convey the message and tone of the story?**
- ⊡ **Is there consistency from page to page and spread to spread?**
- ☐ Are design decisions being made to enhance the importance and clarity of the content, but at the expense of the publication's personality?
- ☐ Are you straying unneccesarily from your publication's style manual – just this once – for dubious immediate editorial success?
- ☐ Are contrasts so numerous that unity is harmed?
- ☐ Does the design call attention to itself rather than reveal the content?
- ☐ Have holes been filled with cluttering garbage?
- ☐ Do elements interrupt reading or cause confusion?
- ☐ Does the shape of any element look contrived or forced?
- ☐ Do elements try to outshout each other?
- ☐ Is there any way to simplify this design?

Page Architecture

- ☑ Is there a simple and coherent design system?
- ☑ Does presentation make the information more intelligible and valuable?
- ☑ Has all clutter and affect been eliminated?
- ☑ Has the rigid use of a grid limited creativity and expressiveness?
- ☑ Is there characteristic page makeup in patterning and texture?
- ☑ Is the design responsive to substance or is it just surface gloss?
- ☑ Do facing pages appear as spreads?
- ☑ Do stories appear as continuous horizontal entities that happen to be broken into spreads?
- ☑ Are the premium upper-left corner and top section of the page used to maximum effect?
- ☑ Are readers guided naturally and smoothly through the page or story?
- ☑ Does your overall design acknowledge the presence of and competition from the Web?
- ☑ Are readers guided through information?
- ☑ Are identity signals (logos, sinkage, department layouts) used consistently to reveal the magazine's structure?
- ☑ Is information ranked so uncaring readers can skim?
- ☑ Can the potential reader learn the gist of the story just from the display material?
- ☑ Are starting points easily found?
- ☑ Does the layout accurately communicate the relative importance of the stories on the page?
- ☑ Are stories shown so readers can gauge time, effort, and commitment?
- ☑ Does the cover arouse curiosity and lure the passive?
- ☑ Is there a characteristic cover format that allows flexibility while maintaining uniformity?
- ☐ Does any element lead to an unintended dead end?
- ☐ Does the design look evenly gray with elements too similar in size and treatment?

Type

- ☑ Does the type look like "frozen sound"?
- ☑ Is the type as large and legible as possible?
- ☑ Does typography unify pages without boring sameness?
- ☑ Are there exactly three levels of typography?
- ☑ Are big stories broken into bite-size chunks?
- ☑ Can the copy be edited shorter or listed?
- ☑ Is the logo distinctive, not just set type?
- ☑ Is the logo echoed in the department headings?
- ☑ Is there a distinctive type treatment that is used throughout each feature story?
- ☑ Has the reader been lured into a story by the headline-deck-caption-text progression?
- ☑ Are sidebars used as backdoors into the story?
- ☑ Has all display type (headlines, decks, captions, breaker heads, breakouts, and pull-quotes) been broken for sense?
- ☑ Does information in headlines – rather than cute punning – intrigue the reader?
- ☑ If the headline has to be a topic title, is the reason to read in the deck?
- ☑ Do headlines contain active, positive verbs?
- ☑ Are headlines repeated verbatim on the contents page and cover?
- ☑ Are all-caps restricted to very short headlines?
- ☑ Do decks and captions focus on the significance of the story?
- ☑ Do captions reveal the editorial significance of visually dull photos?
- ☑ Are captions written as display type hooks, to increase curiosity and lead readers to the text?
- ☑ Do font changes signal changes in meaning?
- ☐ Is the reader aware of the act of reading?
- ☐ Have typographic decisions made the type prettier but harder to read?
- ☐ Do headlines and subheads compete for attention rather than lead from one idea to the next?
- ☐ Is the line width for text (about 40–60 characters per line) appropriate for the type size?

Index

Colophon

A colophon is a brief description of a book's typography and production. The first colophon was printed in 1457 – just a few years after Gutenberg first printed with moveable type – by Johann Fust and Peter Schoeffer. Fust & Schoeffer were printers in Mainz, Germany. This colophon was in their Latin *Psalter*.

The Elements of Graphic Design was designed and typeset by Alexander W. White. It was printed by Transcontinental Printing in Canada.

The text face is ITC Quay, designed by David Quay at The Foundry, London, and issued by URW.

Credits

4-5 VW STANISLAV TUMA; **GOLF** UNKNOWN; **SNO DOUBT FONT** RICH STEVENS 3; **SUOMI-YHTIÖ** UNKNOWN; **6-7 DIPSTICK** TOM LICHTENHELD; **XEROX** JAN V. WHITE **8-9 SEVIN** JOE IVEY; **BANK OF BOSTON** UNKNOWN **14-15 CENTRAL PARK** PORT AUTHORITY OF NY **16-17 SENS** UNKNOWN ITALIAN PRINTER; **FORTUNE** LEO LIONNI **18-19 BOTTOM STUDIES** JOHN MORFIS, DEEGAN LUKIENCHUK, LISA NEWINSKI **20-21 H&G** LLOYD ZIFF; **I HEAR** ERIC O'CONNELL PHOTOS **22-23 CHAIRS** ARMIN HOFMANN; **AERIAL SIENA** UNKNOWN **26-27 CATALOGS** UNKNOWN **28-29 PLAKATE, TOP** JAN TSCHICHOLD **30-31 MAP** ANONYMOUS **32-33 OGNI** *IT'S AN ILL WIND THAT BLOWS NOBODY GOOD. THE BABY ALWAYS CRIES.* **34-35 SARA LEE** EUGENE GROSSMAN; **PAUL SIMON** YOLANDA CUOMO **36-37 AMANTES** *LOVERS ARE LUNATICS*; **COUP** *GUST OF WIND* **38-39 NIKE** DARYL McDONALD; **POWERBOSS** TOM ROTH; **ROTTERDAM** UNKNOWN **50-51 DESIGNERS&WRITERS** MICHAEL GERICKE; **BOTTOM STUDIES** BRYAN GABIGA, JUSTIN NEWELL, MICHELLE MALOZZI; **ELECTRA** BILL DAVIS AT MONOTYPE LTD, CHICAGO **52-53 WESPROS** UNKOWN; **2 SPREADS** UNKNOWN; **LAURIE ANDERSON** BRETT YANCY COLLINS; **DIALOG** PETER SMITH **54-55 DERBY** UNKNOWN; **SHOCK** MICHAEL BEIRUT **56-57 PRESSROOM** BRADBURY THOMPSON **58-59 CITIUS** *SWIFTER, HIGHER, STRONGER*; **TRANSMETTEZ** *BRING A HORRIBLE DISEASE TO THE SLIMY PICKPOCKET WHO STOLE MY WALLET*; **SYM40** CARLA BOUTHILLIER **60-61 FLYING** UNKNOWN **62-63 BOTTEGA** *MAN'S "FLY"*; **VIS** STEVE PALUMBO **64-65 CUTS NOSE** HERB LUBALIN; **TRANSPARENT ALPHABET #4** KATIE SCHOFIELD; **WALLPAPER** VICTORIA AND ALBERT MUSEUM; **NEWSPAPER AD** UNKNOWN; **RAGGED RIGHT** TONY SUTTON **68-69 RAUM** KMS TEAM; **BOTTOM STUDIES** AMY TAGLIAMONTI, DARREN McMANUS, JANINE ERHARDT; **MAURICE RAVEL** EMIL WEISS **70-71 QUASE** *PARTIAL TRUTH*; **BOTTOM STUDIES** ERIN HEALY, PETER DUNBAR, ERIC ASKUE, JULIE TAYLOR FLYNN, DAN HORLITZ, DANA ALDRITCH **72-73 THREE HOUSES** CHIP ALLEN; **THREE MORTONS** UNKNOWN **76-77 SAARINEN** GOTTSCHO-SCHLEISNER; **SAMRAT** ISAMU NOGUCHI; **KOLIN** HE OIING HUI **78-79 CITY CENTRE** CESAR PELLI; **THREE CASTLES** MARTIN HURLIMANN **80-81 REMBRANDT** E LESSING ARCHIV FUR KUNST & GESCHICHTE/JOHN ROSS; **ABSOLUT** UNKNOWN **82-83 LOGONE-BIRNI** MARCEL GRIAULE; **CANTON** L'AMBASSADE DE LA COMPAGNIE ORIENTALE; **SMETTILA** *PLEASE STOP YOUR ACTIONS AT ONCE! I AM NOT A MELON WHOSE RIPENESS IS IN DOUBT.* **86-87 PA GENSYN** UNKNOWN **88-89 WATER & PEACE** SUZANNE MORIN **90-91 POLLOCK** ALEXEY BRODOVITCH; **NEW FACE** ROLAND SCHENCK & BRIAN GRIFFIN; **1979** UNKNOWN; **L'ARGENT** UNKNOWN; **NEW TYPE** OSWALDO MIRANDA **92-93 GOSPEL** MICHAEL BIERUT & EMILY HAYES; **10 TIPS** UNKNOWN; **UN TRÉSOR** UNKNOWN; **MOLKEN-BRONN** DDB THE WAY CITY; **GREEN PAGES** KENNETH C. WEHRMAN **94-95 SCULPTURE** MICHAEL R. McSHANE; **INFILL** MICHAEL BIERUT; **MEMORIAL** DON DYER PHOTO **96-97 DOGCAT** UNKNOWN; **L** LUMINOUS/ ADOBE; **BROCHURE** LEO LIONNI; **FLAG** JOSH ROY; **BABY** JUSTIN PIKE; **TRAIN** ARMIN HOFMANN; **PIANO** KAREN I. HIRSCH PHOTO; **M LOGO** HERB LUBALIN; **CHRIST** MASACCIO'S "TRINITY"; **NIKE** UNKNOWN; **G STUDY** AFTER CARL DAIR **98-99 PG&E** ANTONY MILNER; **GLOBALISM(S)** PENTAGRAM NY; **EIGHT BOOKLETS** JAN V. WHITE **102-103 F** UNKNOWN **104-105 HEY VIDEO** ANONYMOUS; **CROSS COUNTRY** CHARLES S. ANDERSON; **EAGLE-THON** CURTIS SCHREIBER; **MASTERS** ROBERTO DE VICQ DE CUMPTICH **106-107 HERMAN MILLER** UNKNOWN; **NIKE** UNKNOWN; **BOTTOM STUDIES** SHARON JACOBSON; SCOT LEFAVOR, MEREDITH KAPLAN **108-109 TCHAIKOVSKY** KUMARI GANGAJU; **TCHAIKOVSKY** ILYSE DAVIS; **PIANO** AVIVA KAPUST; **TEXT STUDIES** PETER CASTELLANO, AMY PUTNICKI, CHRIS SILVA **116-117 ACEGMORTY** ADVERTISING TYPOGRAPHERS ASSOCIATION OF AMERICA **118-119 AUTARKY** *DICTATORSHIP*; **HO LASCIATO** *I LEFT THE BABY ALONE FOR A MINUTE IN THE KITCHEN AND FOUND HIM COVERED WITH FLOUR FROM HEAD TO TOE.* **120-121 NABOKOV** STEPHEN DOYLE; **SENSES?** MARK GEER; **TCHAIKOVSKY** ANNA GUILLOTTE; **DIE** SARA FAZZINO **122-123 DAKOTA** UNKNOWN; **THINK BEFORE** MARK GEER; **NO.5 NO.2** AVIVA KAPUST; **ABSTRACT STUDY** JOSH ROY; **DESCEND** ROB GELB; **FSTR** KEENAN **126-127 SPAGEFOMTIED** ADVERTISING TYPOGRAPHERS ASSOCIATION OF AMERICA **128-129 STUDENT EXERCISE** CHIRAG BHAKTA **130-131 DODGE** UNKNOWN

Books from Allworth Press

Inside the Business of Graphic Design: 60 Leaders Share Their Secrets of Success By Catharine Fishel (paperback, 6x9, 288 pages, $19.95)

AIGA Professional Practices in Graphic Design: The American Institute of Graphic Arts edited by Tad Crawford (paperback, 6¾x9⅞, 320 pages, $24.95)

Business and Legal Forms for Graphic Designers, Revised Edition by Tad Crawford and Eva Doman Bruck (paperback, 8½x11, 240 pages, includes CD-ROM, $24.95)

The Graphic Designer's Guide to Pricing, Estimating, and Budgeting, Revised Edition by Theo Stephan Williams (paperback, 6¾x9⅞, 208 pages, $19.95)

Careers By Design: A Business Guide for Graphic Designers, Third Edition by Roz Goldfarb (paperback, 6x9, 232 pages, $19.95)

Starting Your Career As a Freelance Illustrator or Graphic Designer, Revised Edition by Michael Fleishman (paperback, 6x9, 272 pages, $19.95)

Licensing Art and Design, Revised Edition by Caryn R. Leland (paperback, 6x9, 128 pages, $16.95)

Graphic Design and Reading: Explorations of an Uneasy Relationship edited by Gunnar Swanson (paperback, 6¾x9⅞, 256 pages, $19.95)

Design Issues: How Graphic Design Informs Society edited by DK Holland (paperback, 6¾x 9⅞, 288 pages, $21.95)

The Education of a Design Entrepreneur edited by Steven Heller (paperback, 6¾x9⅞, 288 pages, $21.95)

The Education of an E-Designer edited by Steven Heller (paperback, 6¾x9⅞, 352 pages, $21.95)

The Education of a Graphic Designer edited by Steven Heller (paperback, 6¾x9⅞, 288 pages, $18.95)

Graphic Design History edited by Steven Heller and Georgette Balance (paperback, 6¾x9⅞, 352 pages, $21.95)

Design Humor: The Art of Graphic Wit by Steven Heller (paperback, 6¾x9⅞, 224 pages, $21.95)

The Graphic Design Reader by Steven Heller (paperback with flaps, 5½x8½, 320 pages, $19.95)

Looking Closer 4: Critical Writings on Graphic Design edited by Michael Bierut, William Drenttel, and Steven Heller (paperback, 6¾x9⅞, 304 pages, $21.95)

Please write to request our free catalog. To order books by credit card, call 1-800-491-2808.

To see our complete catalog on the World Wide Web, or to order online, you can find us at *www.allworth.com.*

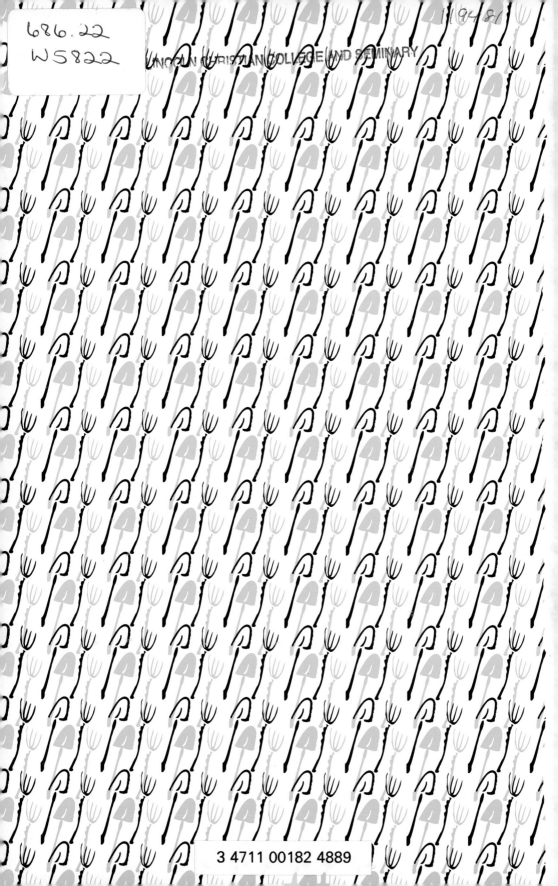